THE ONE-YEAR SCHOOL TURNAROUND

Overcoming School Improvement Barriers Using Common Sense → SOLUTIONS

JAMES YOUNG, EdD

Turnaround Solutions Publishing
4600 Touchton Rd. E., Bldg. 100, Ste. 150
Jacksonville, FL 32246
www.TurnaroundSolutionsPublishing.com

DEDICATION

This book is dedicated to my wife, Sonita, and my children, James, Bryanna, and Timothy; the memory of my mother, Dorothy Young, and grandfather, Timothy Moore; and my mentors Larry Harrison, Ruth Cox, Nancy Snyder, Cheryl Fountain, Afesa Adams, Ken Francis, and Gerlieve Oliver. In addition, I'd like to dedicate this work to the students, parents, faculty, and staff of Pine Estates Elementary, Rufus E. Payne Elementary, Orange Park Junior High, and Jean Ribault High School during my time as principal.

CONTENTS

FROM THE AUTHOR

To: Fellow Educators

One of the toughest responsibilities in education is turning around a struggling school. Throughout the nation, educators are tasked with improving student outcomes on short timelines. A tremendous amount of pressure exists to turn these schools around, most of which is placed upon teachers and school-based administrators. Sadly, certain policies make it more difficult. School choice options allow students to attend higher-achieving schools—leaving the school with even fewer proficient students—standards that increase yearly, and teachers and administrators who receive little to no appreciation and, sometimes, no support.

After an honorable discharge from the United States Marine Corps, I started my career as an educator in 1992. I began my educational career by serving as a teacher assistant supporting physically disabled students in Savannah, Georgia, at the school I attended as an elementary student, R. W. Gasden Elementary. After my time as a teacher assistant and substitute teacher, I taught middle and high school astronomy, biology, earth science, and reading. After serving as a teacher, I became a high school and elementary school assistant principal, eventually leading several schools as a principal.

For thirteen years, I served as a principal at four schools at the elementary, middle, and high school levels. Nine of those years were spent at three schools designated with a school grade of F upon my arrival. All three failing schools improved to grades of A, B, or C within three years. The two elementary schools have sustained, at the time of this book's printing, at least a C school grade for the past ten years. The high school was an F school on "intervene" status, having twelve consecutive years of D and F grades and facing closure. After two years, the school received the first ever C grade, and an A grade was achieved during my third year.

During my time at the three turnaround schools, I worked with many teachers, students, parents, school-based administrators, district administrators, consultants, and state representatives and gained years of experience turning around failing schools. I hope you can use this book as a guide to improve academic outcomes at your schools. Strategies contained in this book will provide aid as you develop policies, create school improvement plans, and turn around your school.

After serving as a principal, I started Turnaround Solutions Incorporated to assist schools throughout the country to improve student outcomes. Turnaround Solutions specializes in turning around schools using common sense strategies and sustaining improvement in one year. We offer educational consulting, program evaluation, seminars, workshops, keynote addresses, and leadership coaching.

I commend you for your efforts. I know firsthand that what you do is the toughest and most underappreciated job in education.

Sincerely,
James Young, EdD
President and CEO
Turnaround Solutions, Inc.
TurnaroundSolutionsInc.com
jyoung@turnaroundsolutionsinc.com
(904) 504-7299

INTRODUCTION

There is a Solution to School Turnaround

It is an unfortunate reality that some schools have failed for so many years they reach the point of having only one year to improve student performance significantly to avoid closure, conversion to a charter school, or management by an educational management organization.

This book focuses on strategies to improve academic performance in schools in one year and barriers that hinder schools from improving. As a principal, I was fortunate to have the opportunity to lead three failing schools. When I became principal, each school had a school grade of F and none had achieved a letter grade above a D. After three years, each school received at least a C grade and sustained at least an average level of performance. The first school received its first ever C grade the third year. The second school received a C the first year and a B the third year. The third school had received twelve consecutive D and F grades. This school achieved its first C the second year and an A grade the third year. The improvement of these schools occurred with basically the same students, parents, inexperienced instructors, technology, and level of poverty.

When I use the phrase "the one-year school turnaround" I am not referencing moving from a failing school to a high-achieving school in one year; I am referring to improving school performance significantly in one year and establishing sustainability within three years.

Turning around low-performing schools is not as difficult as experts make it out to be. The primary reason most turnaround schools never escape the turnaround realm is often caused by the very individuals tasked with improving the school. Billions of dollars are spent nationally in an effort to improve performance of low-performing schools. Districts spend millions on curriculum, software, computers, after-school programs, teacher bonuses, and so forth. A large percentage of this money is wasted; at the end of the day, students are still not proficient in math and reading and the school continues to be labeled "failing."

Three turnaround solutions are needed to improve school performance. The three turnaround solutions are an effective principal, quality instruction, and limited outside influence. Above all, the principal is key. These solutions are all relatively inexpensive and can lead to school improvement in less than a year.

The principal is responsible for creating a culture of high achievement, developing an improvement plan, instilling self-motivation in students, monitoring and managing data, motivating teachers, and providing quality professional development. Without an effective principal, the school will stay in turnaround status.

Quality instruction is essential to school turnaround. A school can have all the great programs, innovative software, fancy computers, and the newest curricula, but if the individual teachers are not delivering quality instruction, students' academic outcomes will not improve. At my last school, Jean Ribault High School, we had five different intensive reading programs and had a reading proficiency of 15 percent. That equals 3 percent proficiency per program and millions of dollars wasted. I tasked my reading coaches and the ELA instructors and intensive reading teachers to develop a curriculum that best fit the needs of our students. Reading proficiency improved from 15 to 31 percent in that year, which was close to the highest reading proficiency increase in the state.

The toughest obstacle I had to overcome at my three failing schools was not low-performing students, inexperienced instructors, lack of family involvement, or poverty. My greatest obstacle was outside influence. The outside influence came from district, federal, and state policies, as well as consultants. At the high school, we moved from an F to an A in three years. I spent a large amount of my time, however, protecting my students and teachers from the negative outside influences, risking my position in the process.

Introduction

As a consultant, I have worked with many turnaround principals handcuffed by district, federal, and state policies and procedures. Many have the ability to lead, but outside influences often hinder them from doing what they feel is best for their schools.

Low-performing students are never part of the problem. Students enter schools on all academic levels. Adults are compensated to ensure students reach standards before moving students to the next grade. So many times this does not happen, and students not achieving standards are passed from one grade to the next without having the academic preparedness needed to succeed. These students stay low performing until they drop out, are labeled as a special education student, receive a certificate of completion, or get a GED. Very few of these students ever walk across the graduation stage holding a standard diploma.

Education is the only industry where low production seems to be acceptable. If the average company does not create a quality product, the company goes out of business. In education, a school can fail for over a decade and everyone from the superintendent, district staff, principals, teachers, academic coaches, and school staff are paid every two weeks and retire thirty years later with a pension.

This does not have to be the case. There should not be a school with a failing grade for more than a year, maybe two if it has new leadership. I understand that it is tough to turn around a failing school. When a school fails, every current student and the rising students have the option to attend a high-performing school due to school choice policies. The next year, the failing school starts with even fewer proficient students than when it received the initial failing grade and is expected to reach at least an average achievement level. Therefore, the only way to stop the failing is for the school to achieve a grade that does not allow students to transfer. This task is extremely difficult with a school filled primarily with nonproficient students, but it can be done. I've done it three times using the strategies in this book.

PART ONE

The 3 P's:
Right Principal
+ Right People
+ Problem Determination

1

CHAPTER ONE
Place the Right Principal

Too many times, districts make the huge mistake of putting the wrong principal in place. Some districts place their lowest-performing principals in failing schools. Some districts place principals in their turnaround schools who have a year or two before retiring, placing them where they believe the principal will do the least damage. These types of decisions are not in the best interest of students. Failing schools do not have two years to continue struggling until the weak principal is removed or retires. Putting weak principals in struggling schools is the best way to ensure the school continues to fail.

A quality principal is the most important element to turning around a school. Without the right principal in place, a failing school will remain a failing school. Finding the right principal is a difficult task, as few principals exist who possess the characteristics of a quality turnaround principal. Most of these characteristics are innate and cannot be taught. The ability to lead a turnaround school either is in them or is not. An average-achieving principal can be made, but the effective turnaround principal is born with the innate skills to lead the process.

CHARACTERISTICS OF A TURNAROUND PRINCIPAL

COMMON SENSE

Common sense is the number one characteristic of an effective turnaround principal. Half of what needs to be done to turn around a school is a matter of common sense. If the principal lacks this all-important trait, the school has no chance to improve. I have met turnaround principals who had no clue how their school grades were calculated and did not have the common sense to find out or get support. How can the principal develop a plan for improvement without knowing what needs to be accomplished?

The Florida accountability system for high schools gives 200 points for the percentage of graduating seniors achieving a certain score on ACT and SAT math and reading. I worked with a first-year principal at a failing school who struggled getting seniors to take the ACT and SAT. The principal decided to give up and start working with only the juniors. He decided not to spend more time getting seniors to take and pass the ACT and SAT. This was not a wise decision, as only current seniors would factor into the school grade and the school had only one year to get off the "failing schools" list. Being on this list meant current students and rising students could choose to attend higher-achieving schools with school-choice scholarships and free transportation. Additionally, it meant the school could face possible closure, conversion to a charter school, or takeover by an educational management company. As predicted, the school received another F. The principal with common sense would have developed different strategies to get current seniors to take the exams while also trying to get as many juniors, whose scores would count the following year, to take the exam.

I have met principals who did not know which teachers were performing and which were not helping students increase student achievement. What results, therefore, is that poor-performing teachers instruct the students who need the most support and count most toward the school's performance. Since these principals didn't know who the high-performing teachers were while developing master schedules in the summer, they placed their best teachers in courses that do not count toward the school's grade or scheduled them to teach courses filled with students who've already passed the state exams. Districts cannot teach common sense, but districts should have a system during the interview process to determine if the principal applicant has the ability to make commonsensical decisions.

CONFIDENT

The confidence level of the effective turnaround principal should be one of cockiness. They must have a confidence level similar to a boxer, not a tennis player. A boxer claims victory before the bout and makes clear that the opponent has no chance of achieving victory (an assertive stance), whereas the tennis player believes they will win the match but will never claim victory prior to the match, as to do so would be disrespectful to the opponent (a passive stance). The principal cannot be passive. If the principal does not believe he or she can turn the school around in one year, it will not happen. The students, staff, and teachers must feed off a confident principal.

I had no doubt I would lead Ribault High to an A grade. The fact that the school received twelve consecutive F and D grades did not affect my level of confidence at all. I chose to leave a middle school with four consecutive A grades. During my farewell luncheon, I proclaimed to the staff that within three years Ribault would be an A school.

At Ribault, during the first faculty meeting, first community meeting, first School Advisory Council meeting, first principal's meeting, and first student assembly, I guaranteed an A. In fact, I purchased a giant flag that pronounced us an A school a year before the students took the test. From the first day I stepped foot on the campus, I claimed an A. I bragged on Ribault everywhere I went. Of course, I faced ridicule claiming an A at Ribault, as very few believed it was possible. Who could blame them? Twelve consecutive F and D grades does not create many believers. I did not care what anyone thought, other than my students and teachers.

Even though Ribault was a failing school, the students, community, and teachers were proud of the school and wanted a principal who was confident the school would become a high-achieving school. My confidence was contagious. The teachers and students began to believe we could earn an A. Students who'd always bragged about Ribault's athletics and history started bragging about Ribault's academics and worked harder to achieve an A.

PRINCIPAL WITH PRINCIPLES

Great turnaround principals have principle. Many times, principals are assigned to failing schools and do not want to be there; they give minimal effort and make every effort to leave. They put forth little to no effort to improve the school. Some principals want to lead a failing school because of the salary. Many districts pay principals of turnaround schools more than principals at average to high-achieving schools. In addition, these schools have bonuses attached to them. It is possible for a turnaround principal to make $20,000 to $35,000 more than principals in the same district, even while the school continues to show no improvement. Many principals don't even believe the school can improve and see placement at a failing school as a punishment or career suicide. Time and time again, while serving my three failing schools, my colleagues would give me their condolences and make statements such as "Just do your time there; get your F grades and get out," "Who did you upset at the district office?" or "I would transfer to another district before I'd go to one of those career killers."

Principals with principles genuinely care about the performance of the school. They work extremely hard to improve student performance. They're excited about leading a failing school and accept the challenge. Principals with principles truly believe the school can turn around. They sacrifice their time and motivate students and teachers. I volunteered for the second and third failing schools. I know a few others who saw the opportunity to lead a failing school as an opportunity to make a difference. Some believed the school could turn around and did what they could do to make a difference. They also defended the efforts of their students and teachers and set high expectations for their schools.

The best scenario is to select a principal who can get the job done and allow the principal to lead the school without interference. If outside support is mandated, then this support should be coordinated so that all the support is aligned and not overwhelming to administrators and teachers.

INNOVATIVE RISK TAKER
It makes little sense for a principal to do what everyone else has tried to do to improve achievement and still end up with a failing grade. Turnaround school principals should be innovative, trying what hasn't been done and willingly accepting when a strategy doesn't work, moving onto the next one. Each school has its own unique characteristics. Even though the school is failing, there is always something effective at the school. A turnaround principal should build strategies based around the areas teachers and

students do well. It's one of the many jobs of the principal to determine what unique strategies, if implemented correctly, will improve student performance based on the makeup of their students and teachers. These strategies do not have to have a direct impact necessarily on student performance. They can have indirect influence on student performance, such as improving attendance, climate, or student motivation.

After twelve consecutive failing grades, I figured I didn't have anything to lose. I tried everything. One of my strategies was to allow teachers, assistant principals, academic coaches, even staff members and students, to come up with unique strategies to improve our school. They had to present their idea or strategy, a plan, and data to support their recommendations. Most of their unique recommendations worked but some flopped. Most of the ideas that did not work were implemented too quickly.

My science department came to me with a unique idea. Their recommendation was that students report to their regular science class and the teachers rotate to teach different units. All of my science teachers had certain units they taught exceptionally well. The science coach developed a schedule where teachers taught units in different classrooms and students reported to their original science class. This idea was very effective. My curriculum staff did not have to spend time changing the students' schedules. Moving students around would have caused too much confusion. The students received instruction from the science teacher with the highest data in that particular unit. It worked. Even though no other department than the science department truly understood their revised schedule, that year we had the highest percentage of students passing the state science exam in the school's history.

EXPERIENCED

In the perfect world, the turnaround principal would have experience improving the performance of multiple failing schools. This is seldom the case, as most principals have not had the opportunity to lead a turnaround school or have not been successful when given the opportunity. If a veteran principal is assigned to a failing school, it helps if that person has had at least some turnaround experience, even as an assistant principal. Many times, districts assign principals to turnaround schools who have had no turnaround experience. This is not in the best interest of the school, but often this is the only option. Because of the lack of successful turnaround principals, often assistant principals are placed in the schools. If an assistant principal is promoted to principal, I do not recommend their first assignment be at a turnaround school, especially a high school, as high schools are the most difficult to turn around.

Districts should develop a plan to develop quality turnaround leaders. Quality assistant principals should be placed with the quality turnaround principal to learn the turnaround process before they are placed. Professional development should be given to build a pool of quality turnaround applicants. Some districts offer turnaround training for their principals and assistant principals. This training, however, is facilitated most often by someone with little or no experience of success in turnaround schools. If the inexperienced principal has to be placed in a turnaround school, the move should happen in the spring, allowing the principal one quarter to develop an understanding of the school instead of placing the new principal in an empty school in the summer. Additionally, this principal should be assigned a mentor.

Fortunately, I had the opportunity to lead four schools (elementary, middle, and high), three of which were failing. These schools improved nine letter grades in total. As a first-year principal, I was placed at an F school. Two years prior, as an assistant principal, I worked with a quality turnaround principal. I also had the opportunity to start this school in the spring while an interim principal was in place. The interim principal was a retired quality turnaround principal and area superintendent who stayed throughout the summer. This was a fantastic opportunity for me to learn from her while developing an understanding of the school.

DECISIVE

Because of the short timeline involved in school turnaround, decisions must be made that will not be popular. The principal who does not have the personality to tell a teacher they must improve or be removed, to move a teacher out of his or her favorite subject or grade level, or to remove a teacher who cannot improve the academic performance of low-performing students has no business being a turnround principal.

In a small turnaround school, situations often arise where only two teachers teach a grade level or subject. Both teachers are responsible for

50 percent of the content area accountability scores, and one teacher is extremely ineffective. That teacher has to be replaced immediately, even if the teacher has been at the school for several years or even if he or she is a thirty-year veteran. This is a tough decision, but the principal's job is to ensure students are learning.

In an average or high-performing school, a struggling teacher can get support throughout the year. Turnaround schools do not have this luxury. It's unfortunate there's no time to support and train an ineffective teacher, especially if it's a teacher willing to work at getting better. This teacher should be removed and placed at a school that has the time to support the teacher. In small schools, one ineffective teacher can cost the school a full letter grade. If a grade of C is mandatory, the school cannot take a chance keeping an instructor who can cause the school to stay in turnaround status. What is best for students must be taken into account. No student should have to go a year with an ineffective teacher, especially low-performing students.

MOTIVATING

The great turnaround principal is also a great motivator. Teachers in turnaround schools need a motivational principal. Teaching at a turnaround school is the toughest, most underappreciated job in education. The turnaround principal position is also tough, but principals earn two to three times more money, so it's not as underappreciated as the instructional positions. When I was in Marine Corps boot camp, it got tough. There were times my fellow recruits and I questioned why we chose the Marines; we wanted to go home, wanted to give up, but our drill instructors had a way of motivating us. My drill instructor had us so motivated we expected to win every event versus the other platoons. We were so confident we would win that it wasn't a big deal when we scored the highest scores on the fitness test, the rifle range, inspections, or combat drills.

The same qualities my drill instructors had are the same qualities of an effective turnaround principal. Teachers question why they chose to work in a failing school and have a class full of low-performing students. The work tires them; they work late, work weekends, and get so little appreciation. The principal has to find a way to keep them motivated.

9

Not to mention, it's so tough to find great teachers who want to teach at turnaround schools. It's imperative to keep the good instructors in your school.

When teachers are motivated, they go the extra mile. At Ribault, I would have anywhere from 60 to 75 percent of my teachers show up on Saturdays and Sundays at no additional pay to plan for instruction. In fact, they'd request the building be open during the weekend so that they could come in and prepare for the next week of instruction. I motivated using many strategies. Many of the strategies were of no cost:

- Listening to teachers
- Respecting teachers
- Giving thanks for going the extra mile
- Not focusing on the negative
- Implementing their ideas

Each principal has to find the strategies that best motivate their teachers. My teachers said what motivated them the most was my confidence in their abilities and my belief that we would become an A school. They appreciated that I took the risk to believe in their capabilities to improve student performance, taking the necessary heat to protect them from outside negative influences.

Principals who cannot motivate their teachers have teachers calling the union when a faculty meeting is extended, if an additional meeting is called, or teacher-planning time is structured. Principals who fail to motivate also have a high turnover rate, which means they have to spend time finding new teachers and have classes covered by substitutes, hindering student performance improvement.

POSITIVE

Every school has an identity. The identity can be positive or negative. Elements that identify schools may include their high academic performance, fine arts, sports, accelerated programs, historical past, or magnet programs. Turnaround schools are identified, most often, by years of failing, fighting, gangs, violence, high dropout rates, and poor attendance. Ribault was identified by a powerful basketball program, its history, and poor academic performance. Both the boys' and girls' basketball teams have one several state titles. As of 2014, the girls' team has ten state titles, winning the last two in 2013 and 2014. The boys' team has played in nine title games, its last appearance in 2014. In the early-to-mid 1980s, Ribault was a national model school. Ribault was featured in *Jet* magazine as one of the nation's top African-American high schools. Unfortunately, when I became principal, Ribault was most known for academic failure. Before Ribault's recent academic success, since Florida initiated the accountability system giving school grades in 1999, Ribault earned twelve consecutive F and D grades from 1998-2010.

One strategy I used to create an academic identity was to purchase the Sword. We were the Mighty Trojans. The Sword was symbolic of academic performance. Students and teachers would touch the Sword for academic power. The Sword would be on the sideline at the football games. I used it to put holes in our rival's T-shirt. Our rival high school even buried a replica of the Sword in a casket at a pep rally. Students took pictures with the Sword. The local newspaper mentioned the Sword in an article when we received the first C in the school's history.

Symbolic leadership does not directly affect student performance; however, symbolic leadership can be used by leaders to motivate followers.

EFFICIENT TIME MANAGER

A good turnaround principal does not spend excessive time on concerns that do not directly influence instruction. I kept conferences to a maximum of fifteen minutes. It doesn't take an hour to tell the parent that you're not changing the decision to put their daughter on the cheerleading squad. After fifteen minutes, I would make my final decision and recommend they contact the district.

Good turnaround principals also delegate managerial tasks to assistant principals and competent staff members. Areas such as discipline, sports, and lunchroom duty were delegated to my assistant principals so that I could keep my focus on instruction. If I could pass on nonacademic tasks, I did. By empowering my assistant principals, they got to the point where they did not want situations to make it to my office. They understood the issue would take my time away from monitoring instruction, so they did their best to find win-win situations.

My secretary also saved me valuable time. She only brought issues to me I had to address and directed the other issues to the appropriate personnel. If students, teachers, or staff members needed me, they could walk in my office. I always had time for them regardless of the issue. Turnaround principals must always have time to support teachers and students, as principals only go as far as teachers and students take them.

If at any point I got behind on tasks that did not impact instruction, I worked late, worked from home, or on weekends.

DEDICATED

The last thing a turnaround school needs is a principal or assistant administrator who doesn't want to be there. Turnaround schools are not meant for everyone, but repeatedly district leadership places administrators at schools who just don't want to work in a turnaround school. As a principal who requested two of the three F schools I led, I can't imagine why an administrator would not want to work in a turnaround school. The principal who doesn't want to be there cannot motivate students and teachers. As discussed earlier, the turnaround principal has to be a motivator. Those who don't want to work in turnaround schools also lack confidence and the ability to lead the school and motivate others.

The administrators who are bold enough to let district leadership know they don't want to work in a turnaround school are often told they don't have a choice. They're told, "go, quit, or be demoted." Therefore, they go and do a poor job, eventually leaving the school and hurting the school in the process. If districts have one year to improve the school's performance and place a principal at the school who doesn't want to be there, they've sent the message that students are not important and might as well start buying plywood to board up the windows, as the school will be closed. As principals need to use common sense, so does district leadership.

Chapter 1
Solution Summary

☑ Districts must choose the right principal.

☑ A quality principal is the most important element to turning around a school.

☑ Principals must display common sense, confidence, principles, and innovation and enter with turnaround experience.

☑ Districts should adopt a plan to develop quality turnaround leaders.

☑ Principals must be decisive, motivating, positive, efficient, and dedicated.

CHAPTER TWO
Select the Right People

Many barriers hinder turnaround schools from improving. Ineffective instructors and assistant administrators are two areas that impede academic growth. Principals are only as good as the people around them. Schools that turnaround in a year have effective teachers, administrators, and academic coaches. Principals must staff the school with effective instructors and remove those who are not effective. Hiring the right people is the most important responsibility of the principal.

CONTENT TEACHERS
Selecting the right content area teachers is essential but extremely difficult. Good teachers are often reluctant to teach at a turnaround school because of all the uncertainty. Often districts move principals in and out, the school faces closure, and outsiders who hold the power to evaluate and remove teachers revolve through the school.

During my principalship at Ribault, the district offered county teachers with proven records of accomplishment anywhere from $12,000 to $20,000 (depending on years of experience) in addition to their regular salaries. Of 8,000 teachers, not one chose to transfer to Ribault.

The final blow was that the district placed all the teachers on a month-to-month contract. As tough as it is to staff a turnaround school, the district implemented a month-to-month policy, which meant teachers were evaluated monthly and if determined to be unsatisfactory during that month, removed. Very few effective instructors were willing to work under this condition. Here again is another example of those in charge making the process of school turnaround more difficult than it has to be.

To be honest, I couldn't blame the teachers. Why leave a school to transfer to a school that may close down, be taken over by a management organization, or have the principal transferred at any time—and, moreover, be placed on a month-to-month contract?

A decision must be made in reference to the veteran teachers. Their data should be reviewed to determine if they should remain at the school. If the data indicate students are not learning, the veteran teacher should be removed. If the data indicate improved student outcomes, they should remain at the school.

It was rare that I recommended a teacher with high performance be removed from the school. One of the worst things a principal can do is keep a teacher with a bad attitude, a complainer, a whiner, one who's not a team player, or a climate killer. Even though they have positive data, they can do more damage than good. These toxic teachers can destroy a good climate. They must also be removed.

ELECTIVE TEACHERS

Care needs to be taken when hiring elective and support teachers. The key to hiring quality support teachers is hiring those willing to embed instructional strategies in their specialized area. Academic coaches can assist these teachers. At Ribault, each of the support teachers had an individual plan to help support the accountability content areas. The elective teachers participated in professional learning communities with the content-area teachers, and they were monitored as all teachers were.

Elective teachers can make a significant difference in student performance. Students go to band, PE, art, ROTC, and similar classes every day. The elective teachers can embed content-area instruction in their classrooms with support from the academic coaches. The band director can teach compare and contrast lessons by comparing and contrasting jazz to classical music. The PE teacher can have students graph and plot their long jump results. The football coach can monitor his players' GPAs, test scores, and tutoring attendance.

My head football coach spent second period every day in one of the ELA classes. He was not there just to be present and manage classroom behavior. He was active instructional support. When the ELA teacher had the students read aloud *Twelve Angry Men*, the head football coach read the part of the bailiff. He also co-taught and worked one-on-one with struggling students.

The media specialist taught a reading class daily for the few high-performing students. A turnaround school usually has at a minimum 80 percent nonproficient students, so most of the instruction is designed for their level of proficiency. It is essential that instruction be differentiated for high-performing students to remain proficient. Moreover, these students deserve rigorous instruction to maintain their high level of proficiency.

My two Marine Corps ROTC instructors also participated in the instructional improvement process. Both spent their planning times in intensive reading classes, providing additional support. They also taught reading strategies in their ROTC classes and monitored their cadets' progress.

SO WHO'S LEFT TO HIRE?

Some teachers just cannot teach low-performing students. These teachers perform adequately if surrounded by proficient students who are academically on grade level, well prepared, and self-motivated. Because of the lack of quality turnaround teachers, turnaround schools have only a few teachers with the ability to improve academic performance in low-performing students. Most turnaround schools have a high percentage of teachers with little to no experience, or they have a poor record of increasing student performance. New teachers want a job, and, thus, are willing to work anywhere.

Since few want to teach in turnaround schools and even fewer are proficient and want to teach in such situations, that leaves ineffective teachers and new teachers. I chose to hire new teachers instead of veteran teachers who lacked adequate performance with low-performing students. I figured I could teach a new teacher how to teach, if they were not intimidated by low-performing students and possessed content knowledge. You can teach teachers how to teach, but you don't have time to teach them content knowledge. I also had very strong academic coaches who could provide job-embedded professional development (e.g., modeling, co-teaching, conferencing). The coaches also served as mentors, visiting the classrooms of the elective teachers daily and facilitating their professional learning communities.

One of the benefits of hiring new teachers is that though they may not teach in effective ways, they are, most often, willing to learn. If new teachers receive adequate support, they have a greater chance of success. Ribault's reading performance doubled with four ELA teachers having a combined total of eighteen months' experience. Two were first-year Teach for America teachers. One was a second-year Teach for America Teacher, and the fourth started in January of the previous year. Essentially, four new teachers increased reading proficiency more than any school in Florida. In fact, the teachers with the highest proficiency in reading, math, and science were all first or second year Teach for America teachers.

CHARACTERISTICS OF TURNAROUND TEACHERS

When I hired teachers, I looked for the following three characteristics:

Content Knowledge: Does the applicant know his or her content? Is the Algebra 1 teacher proficient in Algebra 1? Is the biology teacher proficient in biology? Be careful. Just because a teacher is certified in an area does not mean they are proficient in the content area; all this means is they passed the certification test.

All principals have hired teachers who did not know their content areas. If they don't know the content, they cannot teach it. Do not hire these teachers. If it's determined that a teacher who lacks content knowledge is in a school, they must be removed immediately. Time is of the essence. There is no time to teach content to a teacher. Bear in mind that many times only one or two teachers teach a particular subject, and no one else at the school can help them.

The best way to determine if a teacher is proficient in his or her content area is to have your content-area teachers and coaches participate in the interview process. I also required each applicant to teach a sample lesson in front of the academic coach or the content-area teachers. If the interview was during the school year, the applicant taught the sample lesson in front of students.

Instructional knowledge: There is no teaching without learning. If a teacher has content knowledge and can't transfer this knowledge to the students, they lack instructional knowledge. Unlike content knowledge, instructional knowledge can be taught during the year. Veteran teachers, administrators, academic coaches, and district staff can assist teachers throughout the year to learn instructional strategies. This is why the daily support of teachers by academic coaches is so important in turnaround schools.

Student knowledge: Student knowledge is the ability to understand the total child and a matter of applying common sense. Some of this can be taught, but most of it is an innate trait of an effective teacher. Some teachers just "get it." The teacher that has student knowledge understands education is not the priority for many low-income students. They understand they have students who don't know if they'll eat dinner. They understand there may not be a supportive adult at home. They understand some of these students must tend to younger siblings at home or work a job to help their families and can't do homework. A teacher who makes homework count as a high percentage of these students' grades does not have student knowledge. Some students do go home to two great parents, a study room, and a loving environment—but some don't.

Teachers who possess student knowledge can manage their classrooms. I have had five-foot-tall female teachers with well-managed classes. These same students would go to another class, taught by a six-foot-four male, and be totally out of control. Why do students behave well for one teacher and not another? Student knowledge.

HIRING TIPS:

- Districts should allow principals of turnaround schools to hire their own teachers. Principals should hire the most qualified teachers regardless of experience level.

- Require teachers to conduct sample lessons in front of a content-area specialist and/or students before hiring.

- Include content-area coaches and teachers in the interview process.

- Do a thorough check on data, especially data with low-performing students.

- Be up front during interview about the level of commitment needed from the teacher.

- Hire teachers willing to learn, work hard, remain dedicated, and believe in your vision.

- Hire teachers who understand the cultural differences of students.

- Hire teachers who understand students from low-income families.

HIRING ASSISTANT PRINCIPALS

To turn around a school in a year, the principal must spend at least 80 percent of his or her time leading instruction. Having so many noninstructional responsibilities makes it impossible for the principal to spend the vast majority of his or her time leading instruction. Quality assistant administrators can assist the principals handling those noninstructional tasks, while also supporting instruction.

The principal should select his or her assistant administrators. Being that each principal has a different style of leadership, personality, level of experience, and educational philosophy, who better to select the best assistant principal for the school? Some principals are those similar to me, in that they believe improving culture and climate is 50 percent of the battle. That said, this principal needs to hire assistant principals who are good with people. A principal who lacks math experience would look to hire an assistant principal who has taught math. A principal who is new to an area may want to select an assistant principal who knows the school culture, its climate, and the community.

Too often, district leadership places assistant administrators in turnaround schools. When I became principal at Ribault, I was given six assistant principals and did not have any input in the decision to hire any of them. I started July 1, 2009, and by April 1, 2010, four of the original six assistant principals were no longer at the school. I finished the year with only two of the original six. The reasons for the high turnover varied:

- They lacked the skill set necessary to help me turnaround the school.

- They held an educational philosophy in contrast to mine.

- They just didn't want to work in a turnaround school and were forced to by the district.

This was a major setback, which may have been avoided if I were given the opportunity to choose my assistant administrators. In fact, of the ten assistant principals I had during the three years, I selected one. She was transferred out after one year due to budget cuts.

WHAT TO LOOK FOR IN A QUALITY AP

They want to be there: The worst decision you can make is to hire an assistant administrator who does not want to be there.

They want to be a principal: Assistant principals who want to be principals will learn all they can, work hard, and support the mission.

They have instructional knowledge: Though the principal is the instructional leader, having assistant principals who are competent in accountability content areas is essential. I assigned each of my assistant principals to oversee a specific content area.

They possess a certain skill set the principal lacks or the school needs: The principal has to spend most of his or her time with instruction. Hire assistant principals who can manage discipline, help improve culture and climate, attend to tasks such as payroll, Title 1, sports, the community, and other concerns.

They are creative, independent thinkers: Never hire a yes-man or yes-woman. All they do is agree with everything the principal says to be promoted. Hire independent thinkers who'll say to you that there's a more efficient or productive way to accomplish a goal.

Even though I was not given the opportunity to hire my assistant principals, we were still able to earn an A. Each of the assistant principals who helped Ribault achieve an A possessed a particular skill set that they were very proficient in and were conducive to helping turn around the school. Instead of spending time trying to train my assistant principals to learn new skill sets, I designated their responsibilities based on their current skill sets. Without their assistance, the school would not have improved four letter grades.

HIRING ACADEMIC COACHES

Because turnaround schools have low academic performance, a high percentage of young teachers, and many average-performing and low-performing teachers, an academic coach is a must, especially for the teachers in the accountability classrooms. The only way the school has a chance to improve in a year is if the teachers have intensive professional development by way of daily job-embedded professional development (e.g., modeling, co-teaching, conferencing), assistance-monitoring data, lesson planning, classroom management, and professional development in professional learning communities.

Each accountability area needs an individual coach. A secondary school should have at least one coach for each content area per five teachers. If an ELA department has fourteen teachers, the coach cannot provide effective intensive professional development to all fourteen. If budget restraints do not allow for multiple coaches in the same content area, the coach should spend his or her time with teachers that impact accountability areas. Small elementary schools should, at a minimum, have a reading and a math coach.

COACH HIRING MISTAKES

Coaches are hired with average to below-average data as a teacher or a coach. If an applicant didn't improve academic performance with their students as a teacher or they were a coach at a school that did not show progress, they will not be able to help your teachers improve performance.

Just because a teacher is a good teacher, does not mean they will make a good coach. Many times, coaches are hired because they did a fantastic job as a classroom instructor, but they struggle as coaches, as coaches provide instruction to adults, not students.

Some teachers apply for coaching positions because they think they will not have to work as hard as they did as a teacher. They think they will spend most of their time in the office. A good coach works just as hard as, or even harder than, classroom teachers. Be upfront when you interview and detail expectations.

CHARACTERISTICS OF EFFECTIVE ACADEMIC COACHES:

- They were strong classroom teachers.
- They have a passion for turnaround education.
- They are willing to teach students.
- They are supportive of teachers.
- They support the school's mission and vision.
- They are not yes-men or yes-women.
- They respect teacher differences.
- They research to find strategies to help teachers.
- They have great instructional strategies.
- They have positive attitudes.
- They are innovative and creative.

Chapter 2
Solution Summary

☑ Principals are only as good as the people around them.

☑ Selecting the right content-area teachers is essential but extremely difficult.

☑ The key to hiring quality support teachers is hiring those willing to embed instructional strategies in their specialized areas.

☑ You can teach teachers how to teach, but you don't have time to teach them content knowledge.

☑ Effective turnaround teachers have content, instructional, and student knowledge.

CHAPTER THREE
Determine the Problem

Crucial to turning around a failing school is to determine why the school has been consistently failing. This is a strategy often overlooked. Before determining the root issues of failure, school leaders, district and state staff, and consultants try to fix the problem by changing leadership, removing teachers, bringing in a new curriculum, hiring consultants, or implementing new programs. Millions of dollars are spent unnecessarily while schools continue to fail.

The curriculum many not be the problem. The problem may be the teachers have not been provided the appropriate training. It could be the entire curriculum was not purchased, which means it cannot be implemented with fidelity. The problem could be school administrators are not monitoring implementation. Alternatively, it could be the curriculum is not being used because it's still in the boxes.

Two years before I became principal at my first school, the school received thirty computers to increase reading achievement. A position was also created for a lab facilitator. The facilitator selected was a thirty-five-year veteran at the top of the teacher pay scale. When I first visited the lab, I noticed the computers were in perfect condition. The mouses, keyboards, and headsets looked brand new. I asked the facilitator why the computers appeared never to have been used. He told me that Instructional

Technology had never come to install the software. For two years, the computers sat unused while the facilitator received the highest salary in the building. Not only were the computers never used, the room had been completely remodeled to accommodate the computers and students had never been in the room. I had the lab up and running within two weeks, just by making one phone call. The problem was not the computer program. The problem was school administration never made the effort to get the lab running.

Before making changes, districts should evaluate each school separately to determine its individual needs. Many times, districts use the same improvement plan for each failing school in the district. This is an ineffective strategy as schools have different needs. One school may lack leadership; another may need additional professional development; and another may need additional programs.

While principal at Ribault, two other high schools were in danger of closing. The three principals were told to write an individual improvement plan for each school, as the district had received a sizeable grant. I focused my plan on additional instructors. One of the other principals requested more technology. The third principal requested more programs. After we developed our plans, the district decided we would all implement the same plan. For that year, one school dropped to an F, the other stayed at a D, and we moved up to a C. Developing and implementing an improvement plan without first evaluating the individual needs of the school will not yield the results needed to transform in a year.

BEST TIME TO EVALUATE

The best time to evaluate schools is in the spring, before school lets out for summer. In the spring, everything can be evaluated, as school is still in session. Teachers can be observed, systems reviewed, procedures and programs evaluated, professional development accessed, and the culture and climate measured.

Waiting until the summer is a waste of time in reference to determining why a school is failing. In the summer, there are no students or teachers. Instructional delivery cannot be observed. Systems and procedures cannot be observed. The only data available in the summer are the data from assessments students took back in the spring or fall.

Waiting once the year begins to start the evaluating process in the fall is insanity. It is too late. The administrators and teachers are already hired. All the effective teachers and administrators are gone. Little to no professional development occurs in the summer, and the same instruction that has led to failure the previous years has begun. It is almost impossible to change procedures, programs, and people once the year begins and improve performance by the end of the year.

I had the fortunate opportunity to lead two schools where I was placed at the school in the spring. This was a great opportunity for me to evaluate the schools before I developed the instructional improvement plan. I was able to monitor all of the instructors to determine their strengths and areas in need of improvement. I was able to use this data to determine professional development needs and to determine which teachers were improving learning gains and which teachers should be removed. I was also able to measure the culture and climate of the school, evaluate programs, and observe procedures. Some areas where there was a need for improvement, I was able to start improvement efforts in the spring, before the year was over. At one of the elementary schools, the parent pickup procedure was an issue. Cars were all over the school, and students could not find their parents. The process took thirty minutes for less than seventy students. We developed a revised plan and implemented it before the school year was out. We even had time to revise it a few times until it worked. By having the opportunity to address the needs of several noninstructional areas, I was able to focus more on the instructional areas in the summer and the fall.

HOW TO EVALUATE

To determine effectively why a school is failing involves using several different techniques. The first, and sometimes only, area examined is test data. Test data do not indicate the causes of school failure; test data just indicate the school is failing. Seldom are programs, procedures, climate, motivational strategies, and teacher preparedness observed. To determine effectively why a school is failing, every single aspect of the school has to be examined. Student and parent perceptions, lunchroom procedures, data management, and facility usage are just a few such aspects. The only way to examine all these possible factors is to use several different strategies.

INDIVIDUAL INTERVIEWS

Individual interviews can tell you a lot about a school. Individual interviews should be conducted with administrators, teachers, school staff, students, community members, and parents. Individual interviews produce different results than focus groups. A teacher or a student may be reluctant to discuss certain topics in a group of their peers. For instance, if a teacher is asked, "What are your strengths?" or "Is leadership effective?" there is a much better chance of getting an honest answer in an individual interview than in a focus group. Individual interviews give the individual an opportunity to discuss individual needs, individual strategies, and individual circumstances. I recommend interviewing all teachers, administrators, and support staff individually and a random sample of students, parents, and community members. Interview questions should be developed relevant to the individual school (see "Interview Questions Appendix").

FOCUS GROUPS

Focus groups are also an important way to determine why a school is failing. Focus groups provide the opportunity to meet with an entire department or groups, whereas individual interviews are very time consuming. Individual interviews reveal the thoughts of the individual, while focus groups relate an understanding of the entire group. Some feel more comfortable opening up in focus groups. When several teachers discuss that the problem is the lack of support from leadership, often the reluctant teacher chimes in. Some are even surprised that others are having the same issues and open up.

SURVEYS

Surveys help because some are more likely to answer truthfully when their responses are anonymous. Technology makes it easier for surveys to be taken online, providing immediate results. Keep surveys short. Participation will be limited if the survey takes too long. Choose survey item carefully. Only include items with responses that can actually help improve performance. Also, share the results of the surveys.

The purpose of conducting the interviews, focus groups, and surveys is to use this data to improve academic outcomes. If the data is not going to be used, then don't waste your time and the time of others. Often, the superintendent has made up his or her mind who will be selected as the new principal before he or she hosts a community meeting to solicit community input. Likewise, the principal is not going to change the tardy policy but gives a survey to teachers anyway to make them think they are part of the decision-making process. This type of song and dance is why it's so difficult to get stakeholders to give input. No one wants to provide recommendations and ideas that will not be used. It is better not to request input than to request it and not use it.

To continue receiving quality contributions, it's important to make everyone, especially those who gave input, aware of the data results. It is important that they were listened to and changes were made by way of their involvement. This is also a great way to build confidence. Stakeholders appreciate knowing that their recommendations are not falling on deaf ears. Parents are more likely to be involved knowing they are listened to and that they are a part of the decision-making process.

When I conducted spring interviews, focus groups, and surveys, I reviewed the results with teachers before they left for the summer. When we reconvened in the fall, I again shared the results of the surveys and showed them all changes made by way of their input. Even if I was not in favor of some of their suggestions, I made it my business to change, implement, alter, or modify something they requested. It was their school also, so their input mattered.

OBSERVATIONS

Observations give you the opportunity to evaluate instruction, procedures, systems, and programs in action that can't be determined by looking at schedules, interviews, or surveys. At my first school, I visited the lunchroom and observed that only two classes at a time were in the lunchroom, with ten teacher assistants, and lunch took two and a half hours. There were so many teacher assistants that one just sat at the door and passed out napkins and straws, another opened the milk, one washed down the tables, one told students where to sit, and the remainder stood around talking. This was such a waste of time. By observing the cafeteria, I was able to develop and implement a revised lunch schedule, which cut lunchtime down an hour by adding three more classes to the lunchroom at a time. I also only used four assistants instead of ten in the cafeteria, which allowed the other six assistants to stay in classrooms supporting instruction. Often, determining some of the reasons schools are failing is just as simple as walking around the school in different areas at different times to see areas in need of improvement.

REVIEWING SYSTEMS, PROCEDURES, AND POLICIES

Some areas of a school cannot be evaluated by observations, interviews, and surveys. Areas such as lesson planning, the master schedule, extended learning opportunities, and classroom management need to be reviewed the old fashion way: research. Research is extremely time consuming and tedious, but effective. Researching the influence policies, programs, and systems have on a school requires a systematic plan. The plan should include what needs to be researched, who will conduct the research, and how the information will be collected.

To determine the effectiveness of lesson plans, a team of those who are proficient in writing lesson plans should review the lesson plans of all the teachers. The master schedule should be examined for effectiveness by administrators, counselors, and coaches. A team should work together to determine if the best teachers are teaching the students with the most needs, if all mandatory courses are offered in the schedule, if the same content-area teachers have common planning, if classes are balanced, and so forth. The only way to accomplish this is to dissect the master schedule. After a thorough review of each area, the next step will be to use the findings to develop the improvement plan.

The following is a sample list of some systems, policies, and procedures that can be reviewed:

- Data management
- Assessments
- Professional development
- Classroom management
- Extended learning opportunities
- Teacher and teacher-motivation strategies
- School culture and climate
- Community outreach
- Lunchroom schedule/procedures
- Facility usage

Chapter 3
Solution Summary

☑ Determining why a school is consistently failing is crucial in turning around a failing school.

☑ Before making changes, districts should evaluate each school separately to determine its individual needs.

☑ The best time to evaluate schools is in the spring, before school lets out for summer.

☑ Test data do not indicate the causes of school failure; test data just indicate the school is failing.

☑ To determine effectively why a school is failing involves using various techniques, such as surveys, focus groups, individual teacher interviews, and observations, to review systems, procedures, and policies.

PART TWO

The Solution Equation

CHAPTER FOUR
Practice Accountability Management

To turn around a school in a year, it is essential to determine how the school grade is calculated. I use the term *accountability management* to describe the process I used to maximize a school's grade by strategically working within the state's accountability system. I equate it to a football coach using every legal tactic to win the game. He may change the entire offensive scheme before the game, tell the student body to yell loudly when the other team has the ball, run plays slowly to shave time off the clock, design trick plays, or make posters of last year's losing score and place them all over the locker room the week before the game. In sports, it's called gamesmanship; in turnaround, it's called accountability management.

Understanding one's state accountability system is critical. I've visited schools where the principal only knew the school was failing but could not tell me how the state determined the school's performance. Understanding the accountability system helps schools establish goals, set targets, and take advantage of what they do well.

Below is a sample list of questions the principal should be able to answer:

- What subjects will be assessed?
- When are the assessments given?
- What standards are assessed?

- Which standards are tested most?
- What are the item specifications?
- How many questions are on the assessment?
- Is there a penalty for guessing?
- How much time is given for each exam?
- Are there ways to earn bonus points?
- Can additional points be lost if improvement is not shown?
- Are there caveats that can cause the school to lose a letter grade?
- Can students use calculators?
- How many points can be earned for each area assessed?
- What types of questions are on the test (e.g., short answer, essay, multiple choice)?
- What percentage of students must test?
- How long is the retake period for students absent on test day?
- Which students count toward proficiency?
- Are student gains calculated?
- Is the performance of the lowest-performing students counted additionally?
- Will the scores of English Language Learner students count?
- Will the scores of special needs students count?
- Are accommodations available for students?
- What accommodations are available?
- Must the accommodation be stated in the Individual Educational Plan?
- Must the accommodations be implemented all year?
- Do midyear-enrolled students count?
- Do retained students count?
- What is a passing student score on each assessment?

- What is a passing school score?
- Do factors such as attendance and discipline count toward the grade?

Additional questions for secondary schools:

- How is the graduation rate calculated?
- Are midyear-enrolled seniors counted?
- Do special diplomas and certifications count as graduates?
- Are at-risk students counted additionally?
- Which students count as at-risk graduates?
- What courses are considered accelerated?
- What is a passing score in an accelerated course?
- Which students count in the accelerated calculation?
- What is a passing score on the ACT and SAT?
- Which students count in the postsecondary readiness calculation?

THE 5 STEPS OF ACCOUNTABILITY MANAGEMENT

Step 1: Develop an understanding of the state's accountability system.

Every state has its own accountability system. For this book, Florida's system is used as a reference. In Florida, all schools are given a grade of A, B, C, D, or F. Grades are given based on the percentage of eligible students passing and showing growth in reading, writing, math, US History, and science. A high school's grade also includes its graduation rate, accelerated performance and participation, and postsecondary readiness (reading and math). Middle schools also receive an accelerated performance and participation score.

Schools receiving an F or three consecutive D grades are put on the "failing school" list, commonly referred to as "the list." Each state has a list of schools that have failed to the point that the school faces sanctions. After a certain amount of years on the list a school will eventually have one year to improve performance significantly or face closing, becoming a charter, or being managed by an educational management organization. In most cases, a grade of C indicates the school has made significant improvement.

Step 2: Determine how many points are needed to achieve a passing grade.

In Florida, since 2009, a grade of C would be required to avoid sanctions (435 points for elementary, 560 points for middle, and 870 points for high school).

Elementary:

- Below 395 = F
- 395-434 = D
- 435-494 = C
- 495-525 = B
- 525 or more = A

Middle School:

- Below 445 = F
- 445-489 = D
- 490-559 = C
- 560-589 = B
- 590 or more = A

High School:

- Below 790 = F
- 790-869 = D
- 870-989 = C
- 990-1049 = B
- 1050 or more = A

Keep in mind many states change their accountability system from year to year. Therefore, it's important to keep up with changes annually. Some changes include the addition of subject areas, such as adding US

History. Some states increase the score needed for proficiency and growth, and some states add special education students and ELL students in the calculation. Recently, many states have started using end-of-course exams instead of state assessments.

Important note: As every state has a different accountability system, each state also has different setup rules. In Florida, a school will be dropped a letter grade if the school does not have 25 percent of students passing the reading assessment, the lowest quartile students in math or reading do not show significant progress, or the graduation rate of the at-risk seniors does not increase or reach a certain level. Failure to meet any of these areas will drop the school a letter grade. If an elementary school scored 450 points but the performance of the lower quartile students decreased from 47 to 45, the school will receive a grade of D instead of a C.

Step 3: Review last year's data and recalculate.

After determining how many points are needed to avoid sanctions, the next step is to review last year's data and then recalculate. Last year's data is a great starting point, but it includes scores from students who are no longer at the school and does not include new students. You cannot use last year's data to develop your goals and targets. Therefore, to accurately determine your targets, you must recalculate your data based on current students. For example, if 6th, 7th, and 8th graders had a combined reading proficiency of 40 percent from last year (6th graders 40 percent, 7th graders 30 percent, and 8th graders 50 percent), this does not mean that the school starts the new year at 40 percent reading proficiency. Keep in mind that the 8th graders have moved on to high school and that there is a new group of 6th graders. To recalculate, you must subtract the old 8th grade scores and add the scores of the new 6th graders. Let's say the new 6th graders were 20 percent proficient as 5th graders, then your new score would be 30 percent (6th graders 20 percent, 7th graders 40 percent, and 8th graders 30 percent). This is a negative 10 percent difference. Schools often make the mistake of using last year's data to developed targets.

This step should be developed for each area assessed on the accountability system. If there is an area that cannot be recalculated, such as graduation rate or an area only tested by one grade level, use last's year score but subtract 10 percent to establish a target. This will lower your overall recalculated score, but it's always better to recalculate lower than higher.

Step 4: Determine targets using current data.

Once the current data are determined, the next step is to calculate how many points are needed in each area to reach the target. The target should be the minimum points needed to achieve the level designed by the state, which is a C (435 points) for a Florida elementary school. In Florida, an elementary school is assessed in eight different areas. The example in table 1 indicates the school received 425 points in 2012 (D). Once the score was recalculated at the beginning of the 2013 school year, the score was 387 (F). To achieve the target grade, the school must improve to at least 435 points (C). Since the school needs 435 points to reach the target and the recalculated score was 387 points, the school would need to increase by 48 points. Since there are eight areas assessed to determine the grade, increase each of the eight areas by six points, which would give the school 435 points, if each target is met.

Step 5: Determine how many students are needed to achieve targets.

The next step is to determine how many students are needed to reach each goal. Table 1 indicated that the reading goal for the school is 42 percent. Forty-two percent would equal 126 of the school's 300 tested students. Once the number of students is determined, then the process of drilling down to the exact students becomes necessary. To drill down to determine the target students, individual student data need to be examined. The first step to drilling down is to find all students who were proficient the previous year and which students are closest to proficiency. The target students will be all students with a proficient score from the previous year, and the students that were closest to passing will be added to the proficient group to equal 126 students. These 126 students give the school the best opportunity to reach the target of 42 percent. All students should receive quality instruction, but the target students will be monitored intensively to ensure the school will reach the desired target. This step should be completed for each area assessed in the state accountability system.

Note: I recommend schools increase all targets by 5 percent, in case some target students do not pass the exam. Moreover, extra points will come in handy as your eligible students may differ from what students are in the state's database.

This step helps teachers understand their individual role in improving the school. Telling teachers the school needs to improve two letter grades or improve by 250 points is too vague and seems impossible. Once the reading target and individual students are determined, each teacher should receive their individual reading targets and the names of their target students. If each teacher has 20 students and a target of 42 percent, then each teacher would need nine students to pass the reading exam. The teacher's nine target students should be any student who passed the year before and the students closest to passing. I also allowed teachers to add students to the target group based on current data. Sometimes teachers had enough students who passed the previous year and, to reach their goal, needed to keep all the proficient students proficient. This method created reachable goals for each teacher. Telling a teacher that she needs to ensure nine students pass is more realistic than saying we need to increase 250 points or two letter grades to reach our target.

The same should be done for each area assessed on the state accountability system. Targets can also be developed for academic coaches or assistant administrators. In the example above, the reading coach would have a target of 126 students needed to pass the reading exam.

Table 1 on the next page shows targets for a C school and can easily be made to target a grade of A or B. I always developed targets for A, B, and C and shared them with the entire staff. An A was always my target, and if we fell a bit short, we would at least receive a B or C.

Table 1

Turnaround Elementary 2014 C School TARGETS

Elementary (800-point scale): A = at least 525 points, B = 495 to 524 points, C = 435 to 494 points, D = 395 to 434 points, F = less than 395 points.

	READING	MATH	WRITING	SCIENCE	READING GAINS	MATH GAINS	READING L25	MATH L25	TOTAL
2012 Actual 425–D	40%	39%	69%	40%	58%	66%	58%	55%	425-D
2013 Recalculated 387-D	36%	35%	59%	30%	55%	62%	55%	55%	387-F
2013 Target 435-C 48 points increase *(6 point increase in each area)*	42% 126 Students	41% 123 Students	65% 195 Students	36% 108 Students	61% 183 Students	68% 204 Students	61% 183 Students	61% 183 Students	435-C

300 – TOTAL STUDENTS (who will take test)
100 – 3rd GRADERS
100 – 4th GRADERS
100 – 5th GRADERS

Step 6: Develop a strategic plan.

Next, develop a strategic plan that includes strategies unique to each assessment area.

EXAMPLES:

Graduation

Ribault's graduation rate increased more than any other Florida high school (approximately 20 percent). Most of this accomplishment was due in part to teachers providing better instruction and increased student effort; however, accountability management played a significant role. Any student who drops out of school will count against the school's graduate rate when their peers graduate. Most schools just accept this rule for what it is; we used accountability management.

Our graduation plan included strategies to find the students who were no longer attending school. The plan consisted of making all-calls, asking students to notify us if they knew the whereabouts of these students. In addition, we placed the pictures and names of these students in the cafeteria ("Have You Seen Me?" board). If a student told us the missing student moved to another city, we contacted the school system in that district for verification. If the student was present, we were able to take this student off our roster. If the student was local, we visited the home and tried to convince the student to return to school.

We made the student aware of other graduation options such as charter schools, adult education programs, virtual school, and programs that offered different schedules. If the student was interested in any of these programs, we assisted the student with enrollment, even if it meant transporting the student and the parent to the site. The assistant principal responsible for graduation and the truancy officer were very effective in finding students. We had 250 students on our senior roster. The assistant principal and truancy officer found twenty-five students who we were able to remove from our roster. Our graduation rate increased eight points by using this strategy. In Florida, the graduation rate is doubled, so we received sixteen points from accountability management.

ACT/SAT

Florida, like many states, includes performance on ACT and SAT in the accountability system. Florida does not require students take the ACT or SAT, nor does the state pay for the exams; however, 200 points of the accountability system is for the passing rate of seniors on ACT/SAT (math and reading). The facts that 200 points were on the line and students were not required to take either exam called for accountability management. The first thing I did was raise $20,000 to pay for students to take the exams. With the vast majority of our students not being able to pay, the $20,000 allowed students to take the exams multiple times (some up to six times). Some students had to be strategically motivated to take the exams, as this was not a graduation requirement. I made it mandatory that each senior had to take the ACT or SAT in order to attend prom, Senior Week, and Grad Bash (our annual senior trip to Orlando theme parks). During that year, we improved on the reading and math exams more than any school in the district. In fact, we were the only school to improve in math.

Acceleration

During my last year, schools received 300 points for the percentage of students participating in accelerated courses and passing these courses. Failing schools often do not have the capacity to offer dual enrollment courses, as few students are in accelerated programs. I decided to meet with all the teachers to determine which teachers had master's degrees that could be credentialed in teaching dual enrollment. We had several teachers who could be credentialed. The next step was to convince the teachers to get credentialed to teach the courses. This was relatively simple as the teachers knew it would help us achieve an A; plus, they could use their credentials to teach these courses at the local state college for additional income.

We had several teachers who had the coursework that allowed them to be credentialed. One of the teachers had a law degree. We were able to get her credentialed to teach legal studies. The art teacher had a master's in art and could teach Art History and Humanities. Once all the teachers were credentialed, we included their courses in the master schedule. By offering the courses on campus, we scored 86 percent for accelerated participation, which meant 86% of our eligible students participated in at least one accelerated course. We scored 84 percent for accelerated performance, which was the percentage of students taking an accelerated course and passing it. We had the highest proficiency of all the regular high schools and even outperformed one of the gifted college prep schools in accelerated performance.

Accountability management was also used for reading, math, science, and writing. Even though turning around a school is primarily about improving instruction, motivating, monitoring, and managing data, accountability management can be used to accelerate performance.

Each school has its own unique characteristics. This is why the principal must be allowed to lead without outside interference. The principal knows how the school operates; they know what works for their students and teachers. Principals must be creative, innovative, and willing to use all available resources. Principals must allow administrators and teachers to assist in this process. Once my staff understood the value of accountability management, they started making suggestions.

After Testing

Many states administer state examinations in the spring. Once testing is over, preparation for the next year can begin. After testing, a few weeks still remain in the school year before summer break. This time can be used to start developing skills students need to start the new school year.

After testing, I met with each grade level at my elementary schools and each content area in the middle and high schools. During the meetings, teachers discussed the skills students needed for the next grade level or content area. Teachers developed lesson plans for the students they were projected to have the next school year in the fall. These lessons focused skills the teachers believed were critical to success in the next grade level or content area.

Elementary Example: The fifth grade teachers met and discussed the skills needed for students to start the new school year. Together they developed lesson plans to address these skills. During the last 3 to 6 weeks of the school year, the 5th grade teachers taught the 4th grade students.

Secondary Example: The biology teachers met and discussed the skills students needed to start the new school year. Together they developed lesson plans that addressed these skills. Finally, with 3 to 6 weeks left in the school year, the biology teachers taught the students who'd take Biology 1 in the fall.

Scheduling: Scheduling can be a challenge. The perfect scenario is to have teachers start teaching the students they'll have the upcoming year. The 5th grade teachers should teach the 4th graders, and 3rd grade teachers should teach the 2nd graders. This would free up the 2nd grade teachers to teach the 5th graders standards they struggle in or standards needed for 6th grade. Another version is to develop a schedule that allows for the switch to happen for at least an hour every day. Schools with built-in remediation courses can simply use this time for the switch. A fourth strategy is to have the current teachers who will teach the lessons developed by the teachers the students will have next year or the teachers who will teach the subject the students will have next year.

Not only does this strategy give students and teachers a head start on the following year, it also gives teachers and students an early start on developing positive teacher/student relationships.

25-DAY PLAN

The purpose of the 25-Day Plan is to maximize the last twenty-five days before the state assessment by providing intensive focus on tested standards with the students who have the a strongest likelihood of passing the state assessments. If a school's proficiency percentage is in the single digits, only a few students are projected to pass the state assessment. Using this strategy will help increase overall proficiency.

Step 1: Establish team to develop the plan.

Establish a team to develop the plan to provide intensive remediation. The team should consist of the principal, teacher leaders, assistant administrators, academic coaches, and district content specialists.

Step 2: Identify the students.

Identify the students who have the best opportunity to pass the state assessments. This can be done by examining data from district assessments, teacher developed tests, and state practice exams. Teacher recommendations can also be used. The key is to use data that best correlates with the state assessment. Only select students who are close to proficiency. Students with behavior issues are not recommended, as they may disrupt the environment. If students with behavior issues are allowed to participate and then cause problems, they must behave or be removed immediately.

Step 3: Determine the teachers.

Determine which teachers are best to teach these students. If the schedule permits, a co-teach model can be used, but both teachers must be extremely proficient in the content area tested as determined by data.

The teachers chosen must also be the type of teachers who typically establish positive relationships with students. Do not force teachers to participate. This should be strictly voluntary.

The instructors chosen can also be academic coaches, administrators, or district staff, as long as they are proficient in the tested areas and their schedule allows for them to attend daily.

Step 4: Determine the curriculum.

Determining what will be taught during this time is crucial. From the exam specifications, determine which standards are tested, and from that list, determine which standards are tested most. Lessons should be developed for the standards tested most on the assessments. The next step would be to look at individual student data, determine in what areas each student is closest to developing proficiency, and develop lessons that focus on these areas. Finally, develop a measure to determine program effectiveness. Each lesson should be assessed for effectiveness daily to determine if students are improving.

This strategy is not designed to teach standards in which students have little or no proficiency. If the student is 10 percent proficient in number sense, there is little chance remediation will help the student become proficient by testing time. The time will be better spent helping increase areas in which the student is already proficient, in order to increase their test score. If the student is 60 percent proficient, however, in number sense, there is a much better likelihood of the student reaching proficiency within the twenty-five days prior to the test.

Step 5: Develop a schedule.

This enrichment should occur once a day for at least twenty-five days. The enrichment must occur during the regular school day, as this is the time most students will be present (attendance will be impacted if the enrichment is offered before or after school). Different content areas should be offered at different times throughout the day to accommodate students who are in multiple subjects. If possible, only pull students from elective or nontested courses. The enrichment period should last for at least sixty minutes.

Step 6: Notify the students.

Meet with students to explain purpose, schedule changes, and to motivate and encourage. Explain the importance of the assessment and that participation in the program will lead to success on the assessment.

Notify parents that their children will receive additional state assessment preparation and their children were chosen because their data indicated they were very close to proficiency.

Step 7: Review the plan with teachers.
Review the schedule and the plan with all teachers, even those who are not participating in the program, as teachers not participating in the program may have students who may miss a portion of their classes. A part of the plan should include procedures for dealing with student's grades and attendance who may miss a portion of their regular classes.

Step 8: Implement.
Start implementation within twenty-five days of the assessment. Twenty-five days is half of a semester and enough time to have a positive impact. Twenty-five days gives enough time to teach, assess, and reteach. Twenty-five days is also enough time to overcome loss of time if the teacher or student is absent anytime during the intervention. Less than twelve days does not allow for a significant amount of instruction. This strategy will lose its effectiveness if started too early or too late.

Step 9: Monitor.
Monitoring is essential. The principal and administrators should visit the enrichment classrooms daily to monitor program effectiveness. This time can also be used to encourage and motivate students and teachers. If the plan is not working, revise immediately.

Step 10: Celebrate.
At the conclusion of the program, a celebration should be held for the students and teachers to reward them for their extraordinary efforts. Allow the students to participate in the planning of the celebration.

Chapter 4
Solution Summary

☑ Accountability management is used to maximize a school's grade by strategically working within the state's accountability system.

☑ Develop an understanding of the state's accountability system.

☑ Determine how many points is needed to achieve a passing grade.

☑ Review last year's data and recalculate.

☑ Determine targets using current data.

☑ Determine how many students are needed to achieve targets.

CHAPTER FIVE
Know the Big Four

Every school must determine where to devote most of their time and efforts to improve instructional outcomes. For some schools, it is classroom management, for other schools it is professional development, climate or curriculum. To turn around a school, the principal and the leadership team must develop the right combination of strategies to focus their efforts. The year Ribault improved to an A, our primary efforts were focused on professional development, curriculum development, assessments, and remediation.

PROFESSIONAL DEVELOPMENT
Because a turnaround school has so many young teachers and so many teachers who struggle to get students to proficiency, a comprehensive professional development plan should be developed. Just as a struggling reading student has an ELA class, one or sometimes two intensive reading courses, and reading enrichment, so young and struggling teachers should have intensive professional development. The best way to provide intensive professional development is to have academic coaches in the content areas that determine the school's performance. Academic coaches are full teacher allocations and providing them is an additional expense. It is much less expensive, however, to provide coaches than it is to have a national dropout rate of 30 percent.

When teachers participate in focus groups, interviews, or surveys, they often indicate they are not receiving quality professional development. Many claim school leadership requires them to provide instruction and implement programs without the appropriate training. Another popular statement from teachers is that the training is provided by a trainer who is not competent in the area or does a poor job providing the training. Lastly, teachers often report training overload. They receive so much professional development there is no time to implement it all.

Many teachers participate in professional development just to receive in-service points for certification and attend trainings not in alignment with the instructional improvement plan. Repeatedly, districts and principals allow teachers to attend conference trainings that have no impact on improving student academic outcomes. Attending the conference just becomes a free vacation at the school or district's expense. Some principals and districts have done a great job determining which instructors should attend what professional development and developing a system to monitor implementation of the professional development. Some districts even require the teacher to prove implementation of the professional development before in-service points are awarded.

Academic coaches are a must for a school to provide intensive professional development. Principals must select academic coaches skilled in providing professional training and job-embedded professional development. Some coaches spend the majority of their time writing reports, covering classes, and completing administrative tasks. The principal should ensure most of the coach's time is spent providing training and job-embedded professional development. Each coach should also be a member of the leadership team.

Districts should ensure that turnaround schools have coaches. A failing high school needs at least one content-area coach per tested subject. Small elementary schools need at least a reading and a math coach. At Ribault, I was blessed with coaches. I had an instructional coach, two reading coaches, a special needs coach, a math coach, and a science coach.

Professional development needs to be designed based on student data. If data indicate a schoolwide issue with reading vocabulary, then trainings need to be provided on reading vocabulary. Time should be provided for teachers to attend professional development. Creating common planning within the master schedule is an effective way to create time for professional development. Scheduled professional learning communities, before and after school, and Saturdays are also times when teachers can receive professional development. Job-embedded professional development, however, must occur during instructional time.

If training cannot be provided by the school's academic coaches, care should be taken selecting the trainers. Trainers selected for professional development should be competent and deliver training in a way beneficial to teachers.

Teachers should be held accountable to implement the strategies learned in the training. Administrators should monitor training and classrooms to ensure training is implemented and having a positive impact on achievement.

CURRICULUM PROGRAMS

What is taught at a school has everything to do with the outcomes. At Ribault, we had five different reading curricula during my time as principal. We only had six intensive reading teachers. Therefore, we had just as many curricula as teachers. With all these curricula, 85 percent of our students were low-performing students in classes where these curricula were taught.

One of the issues with the curriculum in turnaround schools is that typically districts chose the curriculum for a school without any input from school administration. If effective instruction requires differentiation, should not the curriculum for each school? Turnaround schools should have the curriculum best for the individual school. Since consequences for not improving student performance in turnaround schools are so detrimental (closure, charter school conversion, or management organization takeover), schools should be involved in curriculum decisions. If the school becomes a charter school or educational management organization, both of those organizations will select their own curriculum. It just makes since that the turnaround school should have the curriculum that best fits its needs.

The issue usually is funding. It is convenient and cost effective to purchase the same curriculum for each school. It is not convenient, however, to close a school or convert it to a charter school—and much more expensive to have a management company operate the school.

Districts should include administrators, coaches, and teachers from the failing school in the curriculum selection. So many times the Curriculum and Instruction Department chooses what is best, having never met the students or teachers or visited the school. Sometimes they select curricula that require computers for schools that don't have computers. Now the curriculum sits in a box and is never used or more thousands of dollars are spent to purchase computers and develop infrastructure to accommodate the computers for installation. This process could take months. If the schools are involved, however, they can provide valuable input to avoid these types of issues.

When schools fail, one of the first changes is the curriculum. In some cases, the curriculum is not the reason for students not performing, but districts nationwide spend billions of dollars replacing curricula that would work if implemented correctly.

On the other hand, some districts keep ineffective curricula too long. If reading proficiency has been near less than 10 percent proficient for a decade, adequate support has been provided, and teachers are implementing the curriculum with fidelity, the curriculum should be changed. Once it is determined that the curriculum is not working, districts should immediately choose a different curriculum with input from the school's leadership team.

Regardless of how the curriculum is determined, the curriculum purchased should have a successful record of accomplishment. Some curricula are purchased just because a well-known company or educator created them, they're popular, they're easy to implement, or they're inexpensive. The curriculum chosen must create the desired results in a relatively short period.

QUESTIONS WHEN CONSIDERING CHANGING A CURRICULUM

- Was the curriculum implemented with fidelity?
- Are the students of teachers implementing the curriculum with fidelity improving?
- Was the necessary professional development provided?
- Is instruction monitored by administration?
- Does the school have all the supplies, materials, and infrastructure to implement the curriculum?

- Are other similar schools/districts improving achievement using the curriculum?

TO-DO LIST FOR CHOOSING A NEW CURRICULUM

- District curriculum specialists match proposed company curriculum to state specifications and standards.

- District specialists contact other similar districts for references to determine proposed curriculum effectiveness.

- Districts should purchase the entire product. Many times districts purchase curricula a la carte to save money, thus hindering teachers from fully implementing the program.

- Once the curriculum is selected, provide adequate training. Often districts purchase curriculum and provide little or no training. A plan must be in place to train teachers who transfer to the school midyear.

THE BEST CURRICULUM IS A GOOD TEACHER

Sometimes teachers use the curriculum as the only instructional tool; this is not teaching. Proficient 10th graders can read a script and pass out worksheets. Nor is an educational degree needed to facilitate computer labs and take attendance. Ineffective teachers often use the curriculum as a crutch for their lack of instructional effectiveness. They start on page one of the book and move through the book chapter by chapter and only do what the curriculum instructs them to do. They only use the assessments and strategies recommended by the curriculum. They never provide differentiated instruction and lack the ability to reteach. The most effective teachers use the curriculum as supplemental instruction. Effective teachers do not need an expensive comprehensive curriculum to teach a student math, reading, or science. Teachers improve academic outcomes, not curriculum.

DEVELOP YOUR OWN CURRICULUM

For all of our content-area subjects, we developed our own curricula at Ribault and used the district-appointed curricula as a supplemental resource. Of the five curricula we had for reading, we did not feel that any of them would produce the results needed to improve reading performance fast enough. Three of the programs were in the school while it achieved 15 percent reading proficiency for the prior five years. One was added without adequate training, and the other was developed by the consultants during the school year and had no record of accomplishment.

Who better to develop the curriculum for students than the academic coaches and teachers? They spend the most time with the students. The coaches and teachers spent hours developing the curriculum that best fit the needs our students. Most of the curriculum was developed during common planning in professional learning communities. Time was also used after school and on the weekends.

It was not an easy decision to decide not to use the recommended curricula. After choosing not to use the district and consultant curricula, the teachers and coaches were cited for not doing so and I was evaluated as using poor judgment. The consultant company had issues with me for not mandating the teachers use their unproven curriculum. I had to spend much of my time defending what we were doing and protecting my teachers. After data started indicating we were showing more academic growth than the other schools in the district, we started getting more support from district officials. All of my instructors were on a month-to-month contract and were willing to take the risk, as various district curricula had left the school with thirteen consecutive failing grades. Many failing schools are given more leeway to implement strategies that are different from recommended strategies since they are in danger of closing. I recommend the principal of the school contact district officials to obtain approval to implement different curricula.

In reference to the Common Core State Standards Initiative, schools and districts must be very strategic. Some districts have state assessments that are not aligned with Common Core Standards as of yet but require these standards to be taught in classrooms. For the purposes of the school grade, principals and districts should choose curricula that matches the standards on the state assessment.

ASSESSMENTS

Assessments are essential to determining if students are improving. They can come from many sources. Some assessments are provided by the district. State departments of education provide practice assessments. Districts purchase assessment programs. Assessments are pulled from textbooks. Teachers make their own assessments, and teachers, along with academic coaches, develop assessments in professional learning communities.

Teaching does not occur if learning does not occur. The key to any assessment is that it must assess what is taught. Sometimes teachers teach a unit and give an assessment that does not determine if the information was learned by the students.

Assessments must be in a similar format to the official accountability assessment the students will take. If the accountability assessment does not contain true or false items, then neither should the assessments students take throughout the year. If the state assessment contains short and long answer, essays, gridded response, or multiple choice items, then students should be given assessments that include those type of answers. If the assessments are a mixture of easy, moderate, and rigorous questions, the assessments throughout the year should mimic an array of questions. If the accountability assessments were to be taken online, we developed assessments to be administered on computers, which also required developing a computer lab schedule for teachers to administer the exams.

Other than assessments required by the district, the vast majority of our assessments were developed by teachers and coaches in professional learning communities. Each assessment was developed based on the standards and item specifications given by the Florida Department of Education. All the assessments included questions and answers that would be similar to the actual test. This was not just true for the content-area teachers. Elective teachers also followed this protocol. All of their assessments were similar in nature to the actual test, even though they did not teach subjects assessed on the accountability exam. This approach ensured students would be familiar with the type of questions on the assessment and avoided spending time just before the test teaching students how to complete a gridded response or how to answer a question on a computer.

ENRICHMENT/REMEDIATION

Because failing schools have so many low-performing students, a comprehensive enrichment plan should be developed. Enrichment comes in the form of before-school and after-school tutoring, Saturday school, additional class periods, extended school year, extended school day, pull out, and push in, just to name a few. Millions of dollars are spent each year on enrichment. Here also, money does not necessarily produce results.

Several reasons account for why enrichment programs don't produce the desired results:

- Many times enrichment is offered solely because the money is available. Teachers usually receive their hourly rate for enrichment. Some teachers work twelve hours a week, Monday through Thursday after school. Experienced teachers can earn as much as $50 or more an hour. Earning $50 an hour for ten months would give a teacher an additional $24,000 per year, a substantial income for part-time employment.

- Sometimes the teachers who have the most years of experience are offered the opportunity to work enrichment programs. Seniority should not be a factor in determining which teachers are given these positions. The teacher's ability to improve the performance of low-performing students should be the primary criteria.

- Some districts allow volunteers, for profit, or nonprofit groups to conduct their enrichment programs without first determining if the tutors have the instructional ability to improve student achievement or if their programs have program results. Sometimes these companies hire individuals who've never completed high school and pay them minimum wage to tutor for their companies. Volunteers can help schools, but a volunteer who is not proficient in Algebra 1 should not be tutoring students struggling in Algebra 1.

- Extended school day, extended school year, and additional enrichment periods are a great way to improve academic performance. Many times schools just extend the time and do not provide monitoring, or a curriculum to follow. Nor is data analyzed to determine if the extended time is actually having its desired impact. These additional enrichment periods often evolve into extended school care instead of extended school enrichment. Students watch cartoons, text, watch movies, play games, and sleep. Sometimes the teacher who earns $50 sleeps.

- Students are placed randomly in enrichment classes or placed in these classes by homeroom. Students should be strategically placed in enrichment classes. I placed the top students together with a teacher with a proven record of improving the performance of high-achieving students. Students who struggled in a particular standard were placed with the teachers who had the best data in that standard. Our lowest-performing students were placed together with teachers with proven records of improving the performance of the low-performing students.

- The enrichment does not match the instruction in the classroom. For example, a student may attend tutoring and get more math when the student just struggles with number sense. Sometimes the math tutoring does not even match the standards taught in the classroom. If the enrichment does not match the academic deficits the student has in the classroom, the enrichment needs to be adjusted immediately; otherwise, tutoring is just babysitting.

- The key to successful enrichment is to treat it like regular instruction. Enrichment should be approached just like regular classroom instruction. The principal should create a climate where enrichment is taken seriously. There should be an alignment between enrichment and classroom instruction. Enrichment instructors should be selected with the same scrutiny as regular turnaround teachers are selected. Professional development should be provided to the enrichment instructors. Enrichment should be monitored, and enrichment instructors should be held accountable for progress and performance. Enrichment data should be analyzed in professional learning communities, and strategies to reteach should be developed in areas where progress is not evident.

Chapter 5
Solution Summary

☑ Develop a comprehensive professional development plan.

☑ Assessments are essential to determining if students are improving and come from many sources.

☑ Turnaround schools should have the curriculum best-suited for the individual school.

☑ The best curriculum is a good teacher.

☑ Because failing schools have so many low-performing students, it is necessary to develop, implement, and monitor a comprehensive enrichment plan.

CHAPTER SIX
Utilize the Data

As a school cannot turn around without effective leadership and instruction, neither can it turn around without effective use of data. I've worked with turnaround schools that operate without the use of data. In fact, I've asked some principals for their data and heard, "Give me some time. I need to contact the district to get it." If the principal of a failing school has to contact the district in the middle of the school year for data, another failing year for the school is inevitable.

Some schools have data, but it is not the type of data needed to improve the school. Just knowing that reading proficiency was 15 percent last year does not help. What does help is having the overall reading proficiency and reading gains for each teacher, as well as the proficiency and gains for each subcontent area such as vocabulary and reading comprehension. Schools also should have individual student data.

Some schools continue to use the data from the previous year's assessments well into the school year. This data is outdated. If the students took the state assessment in spring and the first semester is coming to an end, that data are useless. It's almost a year old. I refer to old, outdated data as "stale data." Moreover, it includes data from students who are no longer at the school and does not include data of the school's new students. At most, effective data should not be more than three weeks old.

Some schools with effective data simply don't use it to improve academic outcomes. These schools have fancy data rooms. The teachers have fantastic-looking data folders. The principal has an impressive-looking data notebook. And that's where it ends. This data are just for show or compliance. Collecting data and not using it is a complete waste of time.

DEVELOPING AN EFFECTIVE DATA MANAGEMENT SYSTEM

Each school needs to develop a comprehensive data management system. At Ribault, I developed a data management plan with the help of my assistant principals and academic coaches. It took about two weeks to develop and had to be revised throughout the year.

To develop an effective data management plan, we used the following steps:

Step 1: Data Determination

The first step was to determine what data were needed. We decided that we wanted data from areas that would determine our school grade. The school grade was a combination of reading, math, science, writing, graduation rate, accelerated participation, accelerated performance, and SAT/ACT passing rates. We also needed data that indirectly affected student outcomes such as attendance, discipline, and enrichment opportunity attendance.

Often schools collect data that has absolutely nothing to do with student achievement. To turn around a school in one year, there is no time to collect data that will not assist in increasing the school's grade. The primary objective is to get the school off the list in one year. Collecting data that will not have an immediate impact on student outcomes in a year can wait until the school is out of danger of failing. Data such as how many students are participating in extracurricular activities is important, but this type of data will be needed when the school is ready to become a high-achieving school.

Step 2: Data Collection

After we determined our necessary data, we needed a system to gather the data. We assigned certain individuals to be responsible for collecting the data. The science coach was responsible for collecting all the science data. The science coach and science teachers developed curricula maps and instructional focus calendars. The science team determined what standards would be assessed and when the assessments would be given. To determine which standards needed to be assessed, the team simply reviewed the standards and item specification for the assessments given by the department of education. They developed biweekly mini-assessments and some of the larger assessments. As a turnaround school, we were also required to use district-developed quarterly assessments. When students took the assessments, the science coach collected and compiled the data and reported at leadership meetings. This process was also used for math, reading, and writing.

Data for the other areas were assigned to administrators. Graduation rate was assigned to an assistant principal. The assistant principal established a team to assist in gathering graduation data. The team met every two weeks. Each member of the team was assigned to students who were not on track to graduate on time. Each member determined what needed to be accomplished by the students to graduate on time. Some students needed to improve their GPA; some needed to take additional courses; some had still not passed the state assessment. At each weekly meeting, the team reviewed the progress made by each of these students. The administrator compiled this data and reported at leadership meetings. This process was used, as well, for acceleration, postsecondary readiness, attendance, discipline, and enrichment participation.

Step 3: Data Chats

Once the data were collected, the next step was to share the data. Each team leader reviewed the individual data with each teacher. Team data were shared during professional learning communities. For areas such as graduation rates, the teachers assigned to each student reviewed progress with the student. Administrators and coaches also reported data results to the leadership team. These data were posted in the principal's conference room. Parents were invited to the school quarterly to review their child's data, and each month data were presented to the community. Overall, school data were also shared with teachers at faculty meetings.

Students: Most students in turnaround schools are not aware of their individual data. Some don't even know they attend a failing school. As principal, I randomly asked students what their state reading or math scores were from last year. Most replied, "I don't know." It's essential that students are aware of their individual data to turn a school around.

We established Data Chat Days each quarter. I brought in substitutes to cover for teachers so that they could conduct detailed data chats with each individual student and make recommendations for improvement. These chats happened in the classroom while the substitute monitored the class. The teachers met separately with each individual student to review their data and make recommendations for improvement. This time was also used to build student/teacher relationships.

My assistant principal developed what she called Chat and Chew. She was responsible for our exceptional student department. She prepared lunch for her special education students and teachers. Then the students reported to the library and ate lunch with their teacher while they reviewed their data.

Teacher Data Chats: As important as it is to review individual data with each student, the same applies to teachers. Administration conducted data chats with each teacher. Each administrator was responsible for a particular content area. I was responsible for ELA and Intensive Reading. I met with each teacher separately and reviewed their data that indicated areas where targets were being met or exceeded. We also discussed targets that weren't being met and discussed strategies for improvement.

I also conducted data chats with the academic coaches, meeting with each coach separately. This served three purposes: 1) By meeting with all the coaches, I was able to monitor the school's overall progress. 2) I was able to determine the effectiveness of the coach. 3) The data from each content area were used to develop department and schoolwide professional development.

Parent Data Chats: Parents were invited to the school once a quarter to meet with their child's teachers to review their quarterly progress. Instead of sending quarterly report cards home with students or by mail, parents had to come to school to retrieve the report cards and meet with the teachers. Meetings occurred after school and Saturdays. Report cards were sent to parents who did not attend. Students whose parents did attend received extra credit in the form of five points added to the final average of the subject of their choice.

Community Data Chats: Community Data Chats were conducted quarterly. These quarterly meetings were called The Principal's Power Hour. I thought it was important that the community was kept abreast of our progress. At the meeting, I gave a general overview of our data. My assistant principals gave data on nonacademic areas such as attendance, discipline, and enrollment. The academic coaches gave content-specific data results. The Principal's Power Hour was also a great way to foster community involvement and assure the community we were working hard to improve the image of our school.

Step 4: Data Utilization

Using data to drive instruction is the key to turning around a failing school. This process is extremely time consuming, yet essential. Sometimes tough decisions must be made based on data. While monitoring data, we determined we had teachers whose data indicated students were not learning. Most of these teachers were wonderful people. They were loyal to Ribault for years, loved by the students, and respected by the teachers. They went to all the sporting events, volunteered to sponsor clubs, worked late, and worked weekends. For years, however, their students show little or no academic progress. Turnaround is not about nice teachers; it is about academically effective teachers. Because we had so little time to turn the school around, I had to remove those teachers. It was my job as principal to put the best teachers available in front of my students. These are always tough decisions. If the data indicated the teacher was ineffective, I recommended removal.

To use data effectively to improve student outcomes, data must be monitored often, and this data should be used to drive instruction. The problem with most turnaround schools is not that the data are not there but that the data are not used effectively. At Ribault, we met weekly and made modifications. If the data indicated that most students were not proficient on a particular standard, we modified the lessons, retaught, and examined the results again. If the data indicated most students were proficient, then we would send those students who struggled to the teacher who had the best data on that particular standard. Because we had all of our same content-area classes next door to each other, we simply told those students to report to that particular teacher until further notice, and that teacher worked with those students. We did not officially change schedules. After the students obtained proficiency, they were told to return to their regular classrooms.

If the data indicated students were not making progress, the team revised their instructional strategies and retaught the standards. If it was determined that only a few students were not reaching standards, plans were developed for those students while the proficient students moved on. We sat as a team and reviewed this data, using it to revise lesson plans. My reading coach shared the reading data from the most recent reading assessments. If most students were proficient, we moved on. If most were not proficient, the reading coach, along with the teachers, developed a plan of action during their weekly professional learning community. The reading team also developed a plan for the individuals who were not proficient.

Chapter 6
Solution Summary

- ☑ Using data to drive instruction is the key to turning around a failing school.

- ☑ Determine what data should be collected.

- ☑ Develop a system to collect data.

- ☑ Conduct data chats with students, teachers, parents, and the community.

- ☑ Develop a plan to use data to improve academic outcomes.

CHAPTER SEVEN
Encourage Self-Motivating Students

Once we received the C grade the second year, it was a wonderful time for the students, parents, community, and school staff. The thirteen years of consecutive failing grades were over. Everyone was excited, but I knew we could earn an A. I also knew that we needed to do something different to make an A. I believed my staff and I had maxed out our efforts the first two years. Had we continued following the same plan, we might have gotten lucky the next year and made a B, or we could have easily dropped back to a D or F. To earn an A, I decided to focus more of our efforts on developing student self-motivation. I figured if we could empower the students to be self-motivated, we were more likely to reach our goal of becoming an A school.

The two-year journey from F to C involved the teachers forcing students to work harder. We mandated students come to tutoring. As principal, I threatened the cancellation of fun activities such as pep rallies, dances, and Grad Bash (the annual senior student trip to Orlando theme parks) if students did not work hard and give their best efforts. We did have some self-motivated students, but the vast majority worked hard because of our guidance. In order to achieve our goal, we needed the students to want it and work hard without us pushing them.

I decided to develop a schoolwide plan to instill self-motivation in each student. As principal, I believed that if the students were self-motivated it would be easier to help them reach their academic potential. If students were self-motivated, they would take school seriously, work harder, and study more. I also wanted to ensure the students were prepared for life after high school. When students graduate, they will not have the support they have as high school students. Instilling self-motivating traits give them a better chance to be successful after high school.

WHAT IS SELF-MOTIVATION?

BusinessDictionary.com defines *self-motivation* as the "ability to do what needs to be done, without influence from other people or situations. People with self-motivation can find a reason and strength to complete a task, even when challenged, without giving up or needing another to encourage them."

ALL TEENAGERS ARE SELF-MOTIVATED

Everyone is born with self-motivation. The problem is that often the self-motivation of a teenager is not geared toward a significant goal that will bring about the results needed to be successful. Teenagers are self-motivated to do what they want to do. There is seldom an issue with a teenager being self-motivated to eat, acquire a cell phone, listen to music, watch TV, belong to a peer group, or simply survive. The issue is too many African-American teenagers from low-income neighborhoods are not self-motivated to reach their academic potential or work hard to be successful. The vast majority of the students at my school were African-American students from low-income neighborhoods. Many lived in drug-infested, crime-riddled neighborhoods. Most came from broken families without the presence of a father. The structure of the home did not accommodate academic self-motivation.

FROM WHERE DOES ACADEMIC SELF-MOTIVATION DERIVE?

Most teenagers who are academically self-motivated had someone to lead them to this point. In most cases, it was the mother, father, a grandparent, or another relative. Somehow, countless numbers of self-motivated students come from adverse home environments. These students are motivated by their environments. Their desire to get out of that environment motivates them to go the extra mile. Therefore, if a teenager is not naturally self-motivated, someone needs to help them become self-motivated. Otherwise, their chances on becoming successful in careers that require self-motivation are extremely slim.

WHY IS SELF-MOTIVATION IMPORTANT?

According to Ed.gov, the official blog of the US Department of Education, reported January 23, 2013, the most recent national graduation data indicate that 78 percent of students are graduating on time and that this percentage is the highest since 1974. In most cases, K-12 school students are motivated by adults to succeed in school and graduate. Even with support from adults, still 22 percent of students do not graduate.

Many students graduate from high school with no self-motivation. No longer are six teachers pushing these students every day. Therefore, it's critical that students graduate with self-motivation. A few postgraduate opportunities exist, however, that continue to push teenagers. The military is a prime example of an organization that will push a teenager who lacks self-motivation. I am a Marine (once a Marine, always a Marine), and when I went to boot camp, I was told when to wake up, when to eat, what to wear, where to sleep, when to study, how to conduct myself, what I needed to do to get promoted, where to go, and where not to go.

College-bound students who are not self-motivated will most likely struggle in college. There is no one to wake them up, no one to make them study, no one to mandate they get additional assistance. Parents will not receive a letter from the school notifying them of the next quiz. Only self-motivated students succeed in college.

High school graduates who are not self-motivated and leave high school without a plan are less likely to reach their full potential, so it's imperative that schools make the effort to instill self-motivation in students.

HOW TO DEVELOP STUDENT SELF-MOTIVATION

My primary goals at the start of the third year was to achieve an A grade by building on the great work from the success of the first two years and to develop self-motivating traits in all my students. To accomplish these goals, I developed a simple four-step process to increase student self-motivation.

Step 1: Educate students on self-motivation.

The first step was to teach the students the meaning and importance of self-motivation. Most teenagers have no clue what self-motivation is, including those who are self-motivated. Nor do many teenagers understand the importance of being self-motivated. This step involved meeting with every class separately. I thought, as the principal, I had to meet with each student to start the process. I did not believe hosting a schoolwide student assembly would be effective, as the setting is too large with 1,000 students together. Therefore, I decided to meet with every second period class in my conference room for thirty minutes each. Most of the second period classes had less than twenty students, so the setting was small enough that I had the students' full attention. The process took from three to four weeks and was conducted each quarter with each class. It was extremely time consuming, but I thought it was essential as the principal that I lead the effort. During the meeting, I defined the meaning of *self-motivation* and explained its importance. I asked students for examples of self-motivation and asked if they believed they were self-motivated. During the meetings, I gave students personal and relevant examples of self-motivation, providing the following two examples:

I shared my personal self-motivation story. I told the students I wanted to be a Marine. Without telling my mom, I went to the Marine Corps recruiter to collect the information. The recruiter told me I had to finish high school, pass a written military test (AVSAB), be able to run and do pull-ups, stay out of trouble, not have drugs in my system, and pass the physical. After the meeting with the recruiter, I started training on my own every day. I studied and passed the ASVAB, stayed out of trouble, and worked hard to finish high school. Then I went to boot camp and earned the title United States Marine.

The student who wants to become a professional basketball who does only what the coach demands is not self-motivated. That player is motivated by the coach (similar to a parent telling a child to clean his or her room). The self-motivated player stays after practice and shoots free throws, keeps his grades up in the off season, trains year round, watches films of his previous games to improve, studies professional basketball players, eats healthy, and plays basketball year round without being told by a coach to do so.

The key to this step is to ensure teenagers have an understanding of self-motivation and its relevance to their future and to give the students relevant examples they can apply to themselves. This step can be modified, of course, when working with younger students in elementary and middle schools.

Step 2: Assess and inform students.

The next step was to measure the student's current level of self-motivation. Students took a yes/no self-motivation questionnaire to determine their level of self-motivation. Students answering no to less than five questions were considered self-motivated. Second period teachers reviewed results individually with each student.

1. Do you wake yourself up for school?
2. Do you study at home without being told?
3. If you don't understand something, do you ask a teacher for help?
4. If you have a low grade, do you attend tutoring without being told?
5. Do you hate to miss school?
6. Do you like school?
7. Do you like to take challenging courses without being told?
8. Do you always go the extra mile for success without being told?
9. Do you develop plans to accomplish your goals?
10. If you fail at something, do you keep trying?
11. Do you try to make an A in every course?
12. Do you do more than the teacher requires you to do?
13. If you miss work, do you ask the teacher to make it up?
14. Would you come to school even if it were not the law?
15. Do you have plans after graduation?

The key to this step is to explain the results of the survey to the students so that they are aware of their level of self-motivation.

Step 3: Write an Individual Self-Motivation Plan.

Each student had to write an Individual Self-Motivation Plan. The plans consisted of personal and academic goals and strategies to reach each goal. Once a student created his or her plan, an adult reviewed it with the student to ensure the goals were obtainable and the plan was effective.

The academic goals were essential to my overall plan to become an A school. Having students list strategies to improve their academic outcomes helped improve their performance.

Many of the personal goals were becoming professional athletes, singers, world-renowned fashion designers, and other lofty goals. Even though very few people in the world will ever reach these goals, the purpose of this step was for students to understand self-motivation by setting goals and developing strategies to reach these goals.

The key to this step was to ensure students knew how to develop a personal or academic goal and write an effective action plan. Students will be able to use this process after high school.

Step 4: Provide follow-up, recommendations, and support.

The final step was to provide follow-up, recommendations, and support for both the personal and the academic goals. As with anything else, if it is not monitored, it does not happen. Teachers sat with students and reviewed the students' plans to measure progress. Teachers provided motivation to students not making progress. Teachers assisted students who experienced setbacks with revising their plans. As with adults, teenagers will experience setbacks and will need additional motivation to overcome obstacles.

The key to this step is to support the student through the process.

RESULTS

During the first two years, my staff and I had to force students to take school seriously, give their best efforts, and attend after-school tutoring. As principal, I begged, mandated, and threatened students to work hard. During the third year, we did not have to spend as much time forcing students to work harder. Near the end of the school year, we gave the students the survey again. Most students answered no to fewer questions.

After we implemented the self-motivation plan, we started seeing more signs of students becoming self-motivated. As time progressed, more and more students started attending tutoring voluntarily. In fact, I had to find additional funding to pay for hiring extra teachers to work after school due to the growth in after-school attendance. After football season, players continued coming to after-school tutoring. More students attended Saturday school for additional enrichment to pass the ACT and SAT. More students started requesting advanced courses. Freshman and sophomore students even started asking us to offer more advanced courses for the upcoming year.

Noninstructional areas such as attendance and discipline improved. Because students were self-motivated, they started to miss less days. More students focused on their academics, which left little time for misbehaving in class. More students scheduled meetings with their guidance counselors to request information about college and career opportunities.

In reference to the school grade, we did become an A school. In fact, we were the highest-achieving school in our district of the twenty-two neighborhood high schools. We even outscored some of the academically gifted college prep magnet schools in some areas. We achieved our highest graduation rate ever, increasing from 65 to 85 percent. We also improved more than any school in the district in reading proficiency, graduation rate, acceleration, and postsecondary readiness.

I am often asked, "How did you improve the lowest-performing school in the state to an A school?" Though several factors were involved, the difference during the A year was that the students wanted it. Their level of self-motivation increased. They wanted to do well, not for us but for themselves.

Chapter 7
Solution Summary

☑ Self-motivating students are essential to school turnaround.

☑ Educate students on self-motivation.

☑ Assess and inform the student as to his or her level of self-motivation.

☑ The student should develop an Individual Self-Motivation Plan.

☑ Student self-motivation plans should be reviewed with students by adults.

☑ Provide follow-up, recommendations, and support.

CHAPTER EIGHT

Foster Fun in Work and Learning

Principals must make the school a fun place for teachers to work and students to learn. Teachers are not knocking down the doors to work in turnaround schools. Therefore, principals must do whatever needs to be done to keep the current teachers happy. This has a direct influence on student achievement. A happy place to work decreases turnover rate, which keeps the school from having vacancies. The more vacancies, the more time students are without a quality instructor. A low turnover rate also saves the principal from spending time interviewing and training new teachers. Keeping teachers also saves the district from having to find a new teacher. As with any other profession, happy employees work harder. The same is true for educators in failing schools. Happy teachers also work harder. When teachers hate the working environment, they want to transfer. When they don't feel appreciated, they do not go the extra mile. It is essential to create a positive environment for teachers and staff.

A principal is only as good as the teachers around him or her. The principal must take care of the teachers. Teachers deal with the stress and pressure from working at a failing school, work late and often weekends, and teach a high percentage of low-performing students, so the last thing they need is to work where they don't feel appreciated and hate coming to work. I have spoken with teachers who hated going to work. They'd tell me they dreaded the drive to the school. They sat in the parking lot, trying to gather themselves before entering the school. Just because the school is failing does not mean it cannot be a fun place to work. I had a very low turnover rate at my schools because I created a wonderful working environment, treated my teachers special, and showed them how much I appreciated their efforts.

STRATEGIES FOR TEACHERS AND STAFF

Below is a sample list of things I did to create a positive work environment. Every principal should create their own strategies based on what works for their teachers.

Respect Everyone: At each of my schools, every adult was treated with the same respect. Teachers, cafeteria staff, custodians, administrators were all treated the same. We were equals. In fact, one of my mentors was the custodian at my first school. He was extremely instrumental in helping me get though those first years as a principal. He was the first person I took with me to my second school. Often staff is not treated with the same respect as teachers. Every strategy to increase morale included everyone. The luncheons, appreciation gifts, and activities included all faculty and staff.

Every month must be teacher/staff appreciate month: The principal must find a way to show teachers how much their hard work is appreciated. This does not necessarily involve spending money. Just saying "thank you" is effective. I gave lots of recognition. In my weekly newsletter, I announced when teachers went above and beyond, got accepted into master's and doctorate programs, and received advanced degrees. I announced where their children were accepted into college and when they graduated, when their children completed military boot camp, were promoted, left to serve overseas, or returned home from service. I also posted students' improvement data around the school for the teachers whose low-performing students showed the most improvement. I made announcements on the intercom and told students how wonderful their teachers were, making sure to recognize when teachers went the extra mile for students.

Golden Spikes: I developed a theme for each year. I used the theme "Full Steam Ahead" at both the elementary schools. I went to the railroad and retrieved rusty used railroad spikes. I sanded them down and painted them metallic gold. During monthly faculty and staff meetings, those going above and beyond received the Golden Spike Award. This was an inexpensive way to show appreciation. This strategy was created by the principal at the elementary school where I served as vice principal.

Quarterly Appreciation Cookouts: Every quarter, I held a cookout for the teachers. I actually did the cooking. I sent an email to the staff inviting them to come out to the area during their lunchtime and signed the email, "Chef Young." I purchased a chef hat and jacket and cooked ribs, chicken, fish, and burgers. My assistant principals made all the side items. These cookouts consumed an entire day, which caused me to get behind on my normal principal duties, so I had to go to the school on the weekends to catch up, a very small sacrifice to show teachers appreciation.

Annual Cook-Off: I started an annual cook-off (similar to the show on television). Any staff member could participate. We had teachers, custodians, secretaries, and administrators participating. I also participated. Another group volunteered to judge the dishes. After school, the entire staff gathered in the media center. Each participant was given the opportunity to describe their dish and the judges gave them a critique. When it came time to critique my dish, I always got hammered. They were brutal. It was all in fun, but I knew my dish was the best. The winner received a giant trophy. Because the budget was so tight, the media specialist found a broken trophy and took it to a trophy shop. They repaired the trophy and put a new plate on it. After the contest, the staff ate the meals. This was also another great way for us to bond as a team.

Tennis Tournament: Several of the faculty and staff played tennis— maybe because the staff was so young. Therefore, I started an annual staff tennis tournament. I again participated. For some reason, the staff always cheered for my opponents. The winner received another refurbished trophy.

Pave the Parking Lot: On certain planning days, about an hour or two before the day was over, I'd announce that all cars had to be removed because the parking lot was going to be repaved. Of course, the parking lot was not going to be repaved. This was an opportunity for me to give the teachers an early release. Unbelievably, some teachers and staff moved their cars across the street, not understanding the subliminal message.

Off-Campus Faculty Meetings: At my second elementary school, every other Friday (payday), I announced just before the final bell that we were having an "off-campus staff meeting." Our off-campus staff meetings consisted of the entire staff meeting at a local establishment to unwind and take off our educator hats for a while. These meetings were a wonderful way for us to grow as a team.

Mother's Day Cards: For Mother's Day, I purchased blank Mother's Day cards for every mom within the school. I wrote a personal note and signed each card.

Coffee Breaks: Occasionally, I had my secretaries pick up doughnuts and coffee for the entire staff. The administrative team delivered coffee and doughnuts to the teachers in their classrooms and everyone else in their work areas. While the teachers came to the cart, one of the administrators covered the class. This was just another way to show teachers how much we appreciated their efforts.

Team Wildcat: At Orange Park Junior High (home of the Wildcats), I challenged my teachers to run the annual 15K (9.4 miles). We trained together for months after school and supported each other throughout the training. The day before the race, I gave each teacher a Team Wildcat shirt. After the race, we celebrated together. The first day after the race, I announced all the participants over the intercom and presented each member with an award at the following faculty meeting for completing the race.

Showing Concern for Teachers and Staff: Showing teachers you care about them and respect them is the most effective way to create a happy working environment. If a teacher was out sick, I called to check on them. If they were admitted into the hospital, I visited them. If they left early due to a sick child, I called and checked on the status of the child. I went to the funerals of their loved ones. If a custodian was moving lunch tables or stacking chairs, I assisted.

When teachers are appreciated, they will go the extra mile, stay late, and come in on weekends. My teachers requested the school stay open late and on weekends. My turnover rate at each school was very low and lowered each year. Teachers from the high-performing school called inquiring about vacancies because they heard about how I treated my teachers. When I am asked, "How did you turnaround three failing schools?" The first answer is TEACHERS!

STRATEGIES FOR STUDENTS

Sometimes schools become so caught up in students passing state exams, the fact that students are still children is often forgotten. Elementary, middle, and high school students should improve their academic performance in school but also have fun and lasting positive memories, regardless of the school's accountability performance. Some schools cut out fun activities such as pep rallies to avoid losing that hour of instruction. Is that one hour really going to make a difference in the school's performance? Some schools do not have activities because they believe the students will not behave in unstructured environments. If this is the case, the principal must do a better job of teaching students expectations.

Very few students want to attend a failing school. Principals should make school fun for students, especially at a failing school, as these students do not have to attend. At Ribault, only half of the students in the attendance area attended the school. Most of the students in the attendance area who did not attend Ribault attended other high schools in the district that were not labeled failing.

Because enrollment was so low, I had to ensure school was fun for the students who decide to attend. Developing a plan to make school fun for students was simple. I met with a group of students who represented a sample of the student population. Often adults make the decisions for students, but who better to know how to have fun than the students? The team consisted of some of the highest-performing students, students who got in trouble all the time, popular students, quiet students, athletes, band students, "cool" students, "nerdy" students, and some of the lowest-performing students.

The Students Fun Team made the recommendations for fun. I approved anything they wanted to do (within reason and budget) as long as we met the attendance target, discipline infractions decreased, and achievement on benchmark assessments improved. If the targets were met, the teachers and I made their wishes happen.

SAMPLE STUDENT RECOMMENDATIONS (THAT I APPROVED)

In School Dances: We offered two dances during the school day, within the school year.

More Pep Rallies: We added a few additional pep rallies.

81

Fun Day (all day): Fun Day was a day when students had fun without any instruction. I agreed as long as we increased our school grade. The school grade improved from a D to the first C ever. They requested I grill burgers and fry chicken and fries, and my assistant principal prepare a low country boil (a giant pot full of seafood, potatoes, corn, sausages, and eggs). I purchased and cooked 4,000 chicken wings, 1,000 burgers, and 300 pounds of fries. My assistant principals prepared 100 dozen crabs, 100 pounds of shrimp, 200 ears of corn, 50 pounds of sausage, 40 dozen eggs, and 100 pounds of potatoes. The entire staff assisted with the cooking. We added cotton candy, candy apples, pretzels, slushies, and bounce houses. We also had a DJ and held competitions between the students and the staff (the staff won most events). To this day, when I see graduates, they still talk about that Fun Day.

T-shirts: I gave students a T-shirt each year. The design was created by one of our talented art students. Each shirt had a specific theme. Year one it was "We Believe in Us." Year two was "Proving Everyone Wrong," and year three was "We can C an A." This was another way to help change the perception of the school. For some reason, Ribault was T-shirt happy. During my three-year principalship, I received more than fifty shirts, but not one of the shirts had anything to do with student performance.

Longer Friday Lunches: On selected Fridays, lunch was extended.

Faculty versus Student Basketball Games: The basketball teams played the teachers in front of the entire school.

Cell Phone Days: Students used cell phones during noninstructional time.

Free Tardies: Students received one tardy per quarter without consequences.

Movie Days: Students chose a school-appropriate movie and ate snacks during the movie.

Individual Students: Occasionally, students ask the principal to attend their personal events. Most principals respectfully decline. I accepted all that I could. I attended many recitals and award presentations. My most unique request was to run with a special needs student in the Special Olympics Torch Run. I was tired, but the student was happy. Attending these events also helped me become part of the community and increased family involvement at the school. The parents and community appreciated the extra effort I made for the students. I also visited the hospital if a student was hospitalized.

Most of these activities were relatively inexpensive and all were selected by students. Allowing students to participate in activities ensures students have fun their way instead of the way adults think it is fun. Sometimes principals make promises to students and don't follow through. This is the worst thing a principal can do to deflate student motivation. The more effort a principal makes to support students and teachers, the more academic performance will increase.

Chapter 8
Solution Summary

☑ Principals must make the school a fun place for teachers to work and students to learn.

☑ Showing teachers you care about and respect them is the most effective way to create a happy working environment.

☑ When teachers are appreciated, they'll go the extra mile, stay late, and come in on weekends.

☑ Elementary, middle, and high school students should improve their academic performances in school but also have fun and lasting positive memories, regardless of the school's accountability performance.

☑ Principals should make school fun for students, especially at a failing school, as these students do not have to attend.

PART THREE

Be Part of the Solution

CHAPTER NINE
Minimize Negative Influences

Many point the finger at the repeated poor performance of failing schools at principals, teachers, students, parents, and poverty. Few point the finger at the negative influences cause by federal, state, and local district policies.

TOO MUCH SUPPORT

For a failing school to turnaround in a year, outside interference must be limited. Due to accountability policies, failing schools not only receive support from the district but also often are mandated to receive support from the state department of education and consultants. One major problem is turnaround schools have too much support. Sometimes there's so much support that, ultimately, nothing is accomplished. At one point, my science teachers had to deal with four science coaches. This was the same for each content area assessed on the accountability system. We had a school-based coach (she was great). There was a science coach from the department of education, a science coach from a consultant group, and a district science coach. At one point, my science coach came to me and stated each outside coach wanted her do something in contrast to the other coaches. She was so frustrated. Teachers were getting directives from too many support specialists. One day we'd move in one direction and then another coach would recommend moving in a different direction. This caused confusion and learning was not taking place. I eventually told my science coach to do what she believed would best support our science teachers to increase achievement and ignore the outsiders. That year we had the highest percentage of students at Ribault to achieve proficiency on the state exam.

CONSULTANTS

Due to years of failing grades, consulting companies are often assigned to failing schools. Many districts and state-led educational agencies qualify consultants and allow the schools to determine which consultant best fits their needs. Districts should allow the principal at a turnaround school to participate in the decision-making process in order to lead instruction. By allowing the principal to be a part of the decision, the principal and the consultants can work together as partners to improve student outcomes.

Districts should also be certain to hire consultants with successful records of accomplishment and innovative turnaround strategies. Hiring consultants who use the same material from a decade ago for each school will not lead to improved academic gains. The best consulting companies develop a plan of action only after they have conducted an intensive school audit of all programs.

Districts should hire turnaround partners with consultants who have done the work. Some consulting companies hire those who will work for the least amount. Often their consultants have not worked in failing schools, or they retired years ago and have no recent turnaround experience. Some even hire family members without an educational background. The best way to ensure the consultants are qualified is to request a resume and turnaround experience record for each consultant potentially collaborating with the school.

My science department questioned the credentials of their science consultant. All teachers were on a month-to-month contract and wanted to know if she was an expert in turnaround education and the research behind her recommendations. The questioning led to the consultant believing my teachers were disrespectful. The lead consultant requested I reprimand the teachers for questioning her. I felt that the teachers had every right to question anyone making recommendations for what they implemented in class, as their careers were on the line and were on month-to-month contracts. The consultants also recommended I be removed as principal due to poor leadership and refusal to follow any of their recommendations. My supervisors called me in, issued a reprimand, and insisted I apologize on behalf of the teachers. This situation could have been avoided if the credentials of the consultants were revealed to school leadership and instructors.

HUMAN RESOURCES PROCEDURES

Human resource policies in many districts can help schools in turnaround. This help is especially critical if a teacher has made it clear they no longer want to work at the school but the human resources policy states there is no midyear transfer or the teacher must stay at the school a certain amount of years. Because of the policy, students are stuck with a teacher who does not want to be the instructor. The teacher may give minimum performance until the year ends, but turnaround schools cannot have teachers who do not go above and beyond. Districts that have policies allowing teachers to leave failing schools and have a strong recruitment program truly help student performance. Forcing a teacher to stay at a turnaround school is not in the best interest of student performance.

VACANCIES

High-performing schools sometimes have 300 applicants apply for one vacancy. They have the luxury to select the right candidate. Turnaround schools have vacancies for months, as there are no applicants for the vacancies. Sometimes principals are forced to place a substitute in vacancies for the entire year or hire an applicant who has certification but lacks the skills. Because there's a shortage of quality turnaround instructors, school districts should recruit and create a bank of quality teachers to fill vacancies. Training programs should be created to prepare teachers for the rigors of turnaround. Real incentives should be offered, not just those that give a small bonus or a one-year bonus. My teachers were offered financial incentives until we became a C school. Once we earned a C grade, the incentives stopped and teachers transferred out. Essentially, this incentive program gave schools with slow performance more of a bonus than the schools with fast academic increases. The better my teachers performed, the more their bonus decreased. School districts should also avoid developing procedures such as month-to-month contracts. Few quality instructors would choose employment given such a contract.

UNIONS

I understand the purpose of unions and believe they are necessary to ensure teachers are treated fairly, especially teachers in failing schools. With so many additional demands on teachers in failing schools, unions should ensure there's a balance between the additional work and protection of the teachers' positions. When schools fail to the point that they are faced with sanctions, the opportunity is there to remove ineffective teachers. During the summer, when I first went to Ribault, a team consisting of district staff, union staff, state staff, and myself met to determine which teachers would continue the next school year and which teachers would be removed. After the interviews, I submitted the list of teachers to be removed to my supervisors. Some of the teachers recommended for removal wanted to remain at the school and contacted the union for support. The union put pressure on district staff, and some were allowed to remain at the school. This process was not as effective as it could have been, since the district allowed the teachers to return. Unions should work with districts and school leadership to ensure the best teachers are in front of students.

DISTRICT LEADERSHIP

Sometimes districts are forced to make decisions that may have a negative impact on student achievement. In most cases, districts have complete control over their schools, but when schools fail for many years, state officials, consultants, and management companies become a part of the equation. Often districts make decisions that they would not make if not for sanctions placed on the school from No Child Left Behind (NCLB) policies.

One of the decisions is removal of the principal and instructors. Each year, the decision had to made to remove the turnaround principals or allow them to stay. In reference to Ribault, my supervisors were put in a tough position. They had to make decisions that would show improvement in one year, as state officials and consultants continued to indicate that student performance was not increasing and the school lacked quality leadership.

Because of the all the recommendations, the district had to seriously consider removing me. The failing school policies make it very difficult to lead a failing school. Even though I was not removed, the fact it was even considered affected my ability to lead. This uncertainty hindered my ability to hire teachers, since many candidates wanted the assurance that I would be the principal in the fall. As principal, I had to be honest. As a result, many quality instructors chose not to take the risk to work at the school, as they might have faced a new principal come fall. This uncertainty made it extremely difficult to lead the school. I went to work not knowing if I would be there the next day, on top of the school measuring a 15 percent reading proficiency.

Once the decision is made on the principal, the principal should be given adequate time and support to turn the school around. If there's any doubt in the principal's ability to lead the school, the principal should be removed immediately. Removing the principal is the best scenario for the school and the principal, as the school will not have a potential lame duck principal whose ability to lead, hire, and motivate has been hindered.

CONTINUED SUPPORT

When a school fails, it receives additional support in the form of funding, staffing positions, materials, and other support elements. If the school shows significant increase, the additional support often is moved to another school, and the school falls back to a failing grade the next year. Because of school choice, once the school improves, students throughout the district can decide to attend the school. Many of the students transferring to the school are not proficient. Since the school does not have the additional resources, it becomes difficult to provide the needed services to the additional students, and the school once again finds itself on the failing list. In addition, teachers transfer out since the financial incentives are no longer there. Schools should receive the additional support for at least three years or until academic performance is sustained.

Chapter 9
Solution Summary

☑ Sometimes turnaround schools have so much support that nothing is accomplished.

☑ Once the principal placement decision is made, the principal should be given adequate time and support to turn the school around.

☑ Districts should hire consultants with successful records of accomplishment and innovative turnaround strategies.

☑ Human resources policies should be in the best interest of students, regardless of the policy.

☑ Districts should continue to provide support to turnaround schools even after the school has achieved success.

CHAPTER TEN
Maximize Positive Influences

Once faced with the decision to close Ribault, convert it to a charter school, or select a management organization to operate the school, the school board faced a decision. Their decision was to select neither of those options. Instead, they decided to request an additional year and recommended a fourth option, a turnaround plan developed by the superintendent and his leadership team.

In the summer of 2011, we awaited the commissioner's decision. It seemed to be a long shot that we'd have an additional year without selecting one of the three options. During this time, the unwavering school board put up a fight. They held community meetings in churches to discuss the issues, developed action plans, and prayed for a miracle. They had buttons and T-shirts made in support of an additional year. They attended department of education meetings to fight for an additional year. Ribault's board member protested by vowing to wear white tennis shoes until the decision was made. She and a team of other supporters visited the failing school before daybreak to pray for the schools.

The day before the decision, I started packing my office, as any of the three options would have resulted in new leadership. Later that day, the commissioner of education surprised us with a decision in favor of one more year and allowed the school board's option to be implemented. I am not certain if the actions of the school board and supporters or divine intervention made the difference, but somehow we were granted an additional year. I know their efforts motivated us, and we were determined that their efforts would not be in vain.

The school board was also proactive. During the time Ribault received twelve consecutive failing grades, enrollment decreased, as students were given a school choice option to attend schools that were not failing. Most of the students who chose other schools were proficient students. This made it all but impossible to remove the failing title. To help the school, the board put in two accelerated programs (Early College and IB), which caused some of the proficient students to stay at the school and attracted proficient students to the school from other attendance areas.

DISTRICT
Strategies implemented by the district that aided the turnaround process:

- Human Resources made every effort to ensure no vacancies remained in the failing schools.

- Human Resources was extremely efficient. I could recommend a teacher for hire and the teacher would start the next day.

- Principals had the authority to replace ineffective teachers midyear.

- In the summer, teachers were given the opportunity to transfer if they did not want to continue teaching in a failing school.

- Due to low enrollment each year, our budget was nearly a million dollars short annually, but the district made up the difference.

- Additional curriculum resources were provided upon request.

- Six academic coaches were allocated, which allowed for intensive professional development.

- Five assistant principals were allocated, which allowed me to delegate instructional and managerial tasks.

- A turnaround cluster was developed to support the failing school that included a director, assistant directors, and instructor support staff.

- An efficient Data Management Department provided us with effective assessments and data management.

- The district reduced the number of meetings the turnaround principals had to attend, allowing more time to monitor instruction.

- Teachers were compensated for weekly after-school and Saturday professional development.

- Teachers were given additional compensation for working at the turnaround schools.

- Purchases did not have to go through the normal, time-consuming process. Our invoices were expedited.

- The school day was extended to allow for an additional daily remediation class. This was very important as, at first, very few students attended after-school tutoring. By adding the additional class period, most students were already in school. Having the class second period ensured most students were present, as first period had late-arriving students. This additional period also helped address issues with students who could not attend after-school tutoring because of other after-school programs, sports, or their status as a bus riders.

TEACHERS

Teachers played a positive role in the school's turnaround. Without their efforts, the improvement would have never happened. Teachers accepted the fact that they had to get better. They welcomed professional development, as long as it was relevant. Some stayed hours after school to plan for the next day and worked with struggling students. They requested the school be open on Saturdays and Sundays to work in their classrooms and assist students in need of instructional assistance. The sacrifices of the teachers were countless. They never complained, gave up their personal time, and spent their personal funds to ensure their students were successful.

FAITH-BASED ORGANIZATIONS

Community support was extremely helpful. Directly across the street from Ribault was a church with a pastor who did all he could to help the school. He and his team dedicated certain Sundays to show appreciation for the hard work of the students and teachers. Once we finished testing, he and his team prayed for the scores to improve and to avoid closure. He even hosted luncheons for the teachers and staff during football games. He fought for us with the school board and the students selected him as our commencement speaker. Additionally, three other churches donated funds and sent volunteers to tutor students. Faith-based support played a role in our turnaround.

STUDENTS

Students were the key. Each summer, every student had the opportunity to go to another school. As a failing school, we were mandated to offer opportunity scholarships. Approximately half of the students (900) chose to leave Ribault or not attend. The 900 who chose to stay were determined to make Ribault an A school. They faced ridicule for deciding to attend Ribault, as each had the opportunity to attend a high-achieving school. Instead of leaving to attend an A school, they decided to work hard and make their school an A school. They gave up their lunchtime, stayed after school, and came in on Saturdays for tutoring.

SUPPORT STAFF

The secretaries, teacher assistants, custodians, cafeteria staff, security guards, and truancy officer all went beyond expectations to help Ribault improve. They did their part to ensure teachers and students were successful. The cafeteria staff made sure they got the students to the line quickly to avoid losing instructional time. The custodians stayed later than they were scheduled since students and teachers stayed late for tutoring. One of the custodians volunteered to come in on the weekends to take care of the building for Saturday school. The truancy officer made home visits and counseled students on the importance of attending school. The secretaries did everything they could to support teachers by ensuring their needs were met, the copier always worked, and classroom interruptions were limited. Some secretaries even assisted by helping students graduate on time and providing instructional tutoring. Teacher assistants supported instruction in the classrooms by working one-on-one with students.

ACADEMIC COACHES

The academic coaches had a tough time helping the school. They were tasked with providing intensive professional development to a very inexperienced instructional staff. They researched, created assessments, conducted professional development, modeled, and co-taught. Because academic coaches are considered teachers, they had to ensure they were treated as colleagues and never gave the appearance they were administrators. They also had to find a balance to deal with the state level, consultant, and district academic coaches and still do what was best for student outcomes.

ASSISTANT PRINCIPALS

Without my assistant principals, the high turnaround would never have happened. My assistant principals did a fantastic job keeping issues that did not directly affect student performance away from me so that I could focus my time on instruction. Each also led a particular content area, such as special education, math, science, or social studies. They were responsible for monitoring the instruction in their content areas.

They also provided many intangibles. They came up with clever instructional strategies, teacher and student motivational strategies, and were great with student management. One was a DJ and provided the music at parties. One was a caterer and cooked for the students and staff. One was there for thirty years and provided us the historical perspective, maintenance, and facility support. If something was not working, he could get it fixed within the hour. Two were scheduling wizards who developed master schedules that influenced student performance.

ALUMNI

Ribault was not always a failing school. In the 1970's and 80's Ribault was a national model school. Many graduates from these decades were extremely influential in the community and assisted in the process of turning the school around. The support from alumni was amazing. Even though we were called an "F school," the alumni remained dedicated and determined to see their school again reach high-achieving status. Alumni visited the school and spoke to students. They donated thousands of dollars, brought in recourses such as tutoring programs and scholarships, and sponsored career and health fairs. Some even voiced their concerns with district and state officials, if they believed the school was not getting the needed recourses for improvement or rumors arose regarding school closure.

LOCAL MEDIA

Often failing schools do not consider the local newspaper an ally. Most local newspapers and other media outlets only report negative activity at failing schools. The years of failing grades, the threat of school closings, students leaving to higher-performing schools are subjects of typical articles. This was not the case for Ribault. Though there were articles about the consequences of being a failing school for more than a decade, the local newspaper, the *Florida Times-Union* (T-U), played a significant role in turning around the school. The coverage of the school was perfect. If I were the editor, in fact, there's not much I would have done differently.

Initially, when I was appointed principal, the T-U ran a front-page article about the school receiving new leadership, which included the fact that I'd already turned around two other failing schools. This was very helpful as it gave me some credibility with the students, teachers, and community. The T-U was also present on the first day of school and again wrote another positive front-page article. As community meetings were conducted throughout the year, the T-U covered the meetings and the recommendations from the community groups. When we made the first C ever, we again made the front page, and again when we made the A.

On graduation day, the T-U posted an article on the front page indicating that the state would finally lift Ribault from the state's failing list. The timing could not have been better. I decided I wanted to give the seniors a unique graduation gift. The day of graduation, one of my assistants contacted the T-U and had 200 posters made of the article. Unbeknownst to the students, she placed one poster under each graduate's seat. During the ceremony, I made the audience aware this senior class had made history. These graduates were the first class to graduate from a Ribault not proclaimed "failing" in 25 years. The school had been removed from the failing list because of their efforts. I then had each senior reach under his or her seat, pick up a poster, and celebrate the fact that we were no longer a failing school. The students were so excited. Their families and friends went crazy. I struggled trying to get everyone back under control so that we could continue the ceremony. I'll always be grateful for the positive press given by the *Florida Times-Union*.

Chapter 10
Solution Summary

☑ District leaderships should ensure turnaround schools have the necessary services, resources, and funding and develop procedures to expedite the needs of the schools.

☑ School boards should do their part to ensure turnaround schools have the opportunity to improve.

☑ Alumni support can play a major role in turning around a school.

☑ The local media can have a positive influence on the school's perception.

☑ Outside support from faith-based organizations and community members are essential to school turnaround.

☑ Turning around a school involves the efforts of the entire school community.

CONCLUSION
The Solution Effect

Turning around a school is not as difficult as some make it to be. Again, for the purposes of this book, *turnaround* does not mean improving a failing school to a high-achieving school in one year. *Turnaround* refers to the process of the school moving toward average performance in one year and sustaining performance within three years. I had a relatively easy time turning around three schools within three years using common sense strategies. At Ribault, achieving a C was far more difficult than achieving an A. Because the school had never had a C, very few believed it was possible. Once a C was achieved, making an A was easy—primarily because effective systems were in place and most believed in the vision. In addition, we were a high C school and did not need very many points to make an A.

Overcoming the low performance of students, lack of family involvement, and poverty is the easy part. What makes the turnaround process easier is the district, consultants, and state officials working with schools as partners.

Principals should lead with confidence, creativity, and innovation. They must select the right people, support teachers, and motivate students. Understanding the accountability system, monitoring data, and using that data to provide professional development is crucial. Furthermore, principals must create a culture of high expectations and make the school a fun place to work and learn. The strategies in this book worked for me and were unique to my schools. Principals need to develop their own strategies that work best for them and their schools using the processes outlined in this book.

Districts should not place unnecessary barriers on schools. Instead, districts should select the right principal and allow them to lead. Districts should also make exceptions when it comes to areas such as human resource policies and purchasing procedures. Funding should not be an issue at a turnaround school. Turnaround schools should receive all the necessary resources regardless of budgeting issues. Districts are obliged to make decisions that will improve student performance and remove policies that hinder improvement.

Community members and parents should not accept failing schools. They should be proactive and use their power to support the principal and the school. They should also voice their concerns to district leadership and not accept years of failure.

Consultants and outside evaluators should collaborate with the principal. They should spend more time evaluating all the systems of a school and visiting classrooms before making recommendations.

One-year turnaround is achievable. The key is to use common sense strategies, such as the following, that will have a positive effect on student outcomes:

- Place the Right Principal
- Select the Right People
- Determine the Problem
- Practice Accountability Management
- Utilize the Data
- Encourage Self-Motivating Students
- Foster Fun in Work and Learning
- Minimize Negative Influences
- Maximize Positive Influences

A STORY OF TURNAROUND SUCCESS IN NEWSPRINT

The following newspaper article titles, taken from the *Florida Times-Union* (June 2009 to January 2013), illustrate the struggles, strategies, and successes of one turnaround school.

- June 4, 2009. New principals
- July 17, 2009. Raines, Ribault prep for progress
- July 29, 2009. Raines, Ribault big challenge
- August 25, 2009. Fresh start for youth, schools
- August 21, 2009. 4 Duval schools face closing if no progress
- August 21, 2009. F schools try to keep students from transferring
- September 11, 2009. Residents urged to support schools
- December 8, 2010. High school grades better with new grading method
- January 25, 2011. 4 struggling schools face split possibilities
- May 26, 2011. Raines, Ribault scholars defy intervene status
- Jan 5, 2012. High school riding high on grading system
- June 6, 2012. 3 schools could drop intervene tags
- June 22, 2012. Parents ask questions

- June 23, 2012. Board member: Find principal a job
- June 27, 2012. Ribault principal left to consult; Young says he resigned from school to pursue leadership opportunities
- January 13, 2013. Ribault celebrates an "A"

DATA APPENDIX

JEAN RIBAULT SENIOR HIGH SCHOOL
Performance Indicators
2011-2012

☑ A Grade – Only <u>Nonmagnet</u> High School in Duval to Achieve an A Grade

☑ Only Duval County School to increase at least ONE letter grade each of the last three (3) years

☑ 1088 Total Points – Second (2nd) in Overall Points among Nonmagnet Duval County High Schools

☑ 100 Point Increase in state exam points – Third (3rd) Highest Increase among Duval County High Schools

☑ 623 High School Component Points – Highest among Nonmagnet Duval County High Schools

☑ 65 Bonus Points – Highest among ALL Duval County High Schools

Reading	2011	2012	Increase	Notes
Proficiency	15%	31%	16%	Highest Increase in District
Gains	30%	51%	21%	Fourth (4th) Highest Increase of High Schools
Lower Quartile Gains	40%	61%	21%	Fourth (4th) Highest Increase of High Schools

State Exam Writing	72%	80%	8%	

Algebra 1 EOC	Proficiency	Gains	L25 Gains	Notes
	53%	62%	69%	2012 – 1st year of Algebra 1 EOC

Acceleration	2011	2012	Increase	Notes
Participation	73%	86%	13%	Second (2nd) Highest Percentage and Third (3rd) Highest Increase of District Nonmagnet Schools
Performance	48%	84%	36%	Second (2nd) Highest Percentage Overall and Second (2nd) Highest Increase in District

PSR	2011	2012	Increase	Notes
Reading	54%	77%	23%	Highest Increase in District Highest Percentage (Nonmagnet)
Math	37%	46%	9%	Highest Increase in District

Graduation	2011	2012	Increase	Notes
Florida	66%	80%	14%	Highest Increase in District
NGA	63%	80%	17%	Highest Increase in District
NCLB	59%	75%	16%	Highest Increase in District
Federal	53%	73%	20%	Highest Increase in District
At Risk (4-year)	36%	57%	21%	Second Highest Increase in District

JEAN RIBAULT SENIOR HIGH
2009-2012
Improved School Grade From F to A

State Exam Reading	2009	2012	Increase
Proficiency	18%	31%	13%
Gains	30	51	21%
Lower Quartile Gains	34	61	27%

State Exam Math	2009	2011	Increase	Alg. 1 EOC used 2012
Proficiency	55%	62%	7%	53%
Gains	62%	67%	5%	62%
Lower Quartile Gains	56%	56%	0%	69%

State Exam Writing	2009	2012	Increase
Proficiency	75%	80%	5%

Graduation	2009	2012	Increase
NGA	63%	80%	17%
At-Risk	37%	57%	20%

Acceleration	2009	2012	Increase
Participation	52%	86%	34%
Performance	53%	84%	31%

PSR	2009	2012	Increase	Notes
Reading	50%	77%	27%	Percentages. Includes ALL on-time graduates
Math	25%	46%	21%	Percentages. Includes ALL on-time graduates

James Young, EdD

ORANGE PARK JUNIOR HIGH SCHOOL
2005-2008
School Grade A 2005-2008

State Exam Reading	2005	2008	Increase
Proficiency	60%	68%	8%
Gains	62%	67%	5%
Lower Quartile Gains	73%	77%	4%

State Exam Math	2005	2008	Increase
Proficiency	66%	72%	6%
Gains	78%	82%	4%
	2007	2008	
Lower Quartile Gains	79	87	8%

State Exam Writing	2005	2008	Increase
Proficiency	82%	90%	8%

RUFUS PAYNE ELEMENTARY SCHOOL
2003-2005
Improved School Grade From F to B

State Exam Reading	2003	2005	Increase
Proficiency	43%	57%	14%
Gains	57%	68%	11%
Lower Quartile Gains	57%	70%	13%

State Exam Math	2003	2005	Increase
Proficiency	19%	42%	23%
Gains	60%	76%	16%

State Exam Writing	2005	2008	Increase
Proficiency	39%	82%	43%

PINE ESTATES ELEMENTARY SCHOOL
2001-2003
Improved School Grade From F to C

State Exam Reading	2001	2003	Increase
Proficiency	23%	46%	23%

State Exam Math	2001	2003	Increase
Proficiency	9%	28%	19%

State Exam Writing	2001	2003	Increase
Proficiency	17%	61%	44%

INTERVIEW QUESTIONS APPENDIX

SAMPLE INDIVIDUAL TEACHER INTERVIEW QUESTIONS:

- Do you have adequate resources and materials to provide quality instruction?
- Do you receive the appropriate professional development?
- Does leadership allow you to be creative instructionally?
- Do you feel valued by leadership?
- Is discipline at your school well managed by leadership?
- Does leadership show appreciation to teachers?
- Is the climate and culture conducive to school turnaround?
- Is the vision of the principal clear and concise?
- Is there support for struggling teachers or first-year teachers?
- Is the principal an instructional leader?

SAMPLE STUDENT INTERVIEW QUESTIONS:

- On a scale of 1-10 (with 10 being a love for reading), rate your enjoyment for reading . . . (genre of reading).
- On a scale of 1-10 (with 10 being a love for writing), rate your enjoyment for writing . . . (genre of writing).

- On a scale of 1-10 (with 10 being a love for math), rate your enjoyment for . . . (type of mathematics).
- What do you do when you don't understand?
- Do your teachers care about you as a person?
- Have your teachers provided strategies to increase your reading and math proficiency? If so, what strategies?
- Do your teachers provide you additional assistance?
- Does your school involve your parents in your education?
- Do you know in what academic areas you struggle?
- Does your teacher discuss your data with you?
- Does your school provide social and emotional enrichment?

SAMPLE SUPPORT STAFF INTERVIEW QUESTIONS:

- Does leadership involve you in the instructional process?
- Do you feel as if you are important to the school's success?
- Are you treated as a valued member of the team?
- Do you understand the school's vision and mission?
- Do you think your responsibilities are important to the school's success?

SAMPLE PARENTS INTERVIEW QUESTIONS:

- Does the school communicate effectively with you?
- Do you know if your child is being successful?
- Do you know how to get additional assistance from the school?
- Is the school welcoming to parents?
- Does the school value your support?
- Does the school operate in your child's best interest?

SAMPLE ADMINISTRATOR INTERVIEW QUESTIONS:

- Does district administration support your efforts?
- Are you able to be creative?
- Do you have control in hiring choices?
- Are your assistant principals and academic coaches well trained?
- Do you have the ability to make curriculum decisions?
- Do bureaucracy and politics hinder your performance?
- Does the district provide adequate training?
- Does the district provide adequate funding for you to be successful?
- Is there too much support hindering the turnaround process?
- Do you have the power to make a difference?

TURNAROUND SOLUTIONS, INC.
SERVICES

TurnaroundSolutionsInc.com

Turnaround Solutions, Inc. (TS) specializes in school reform. TS employees a team of educators with decades of experience in education dedicated to improving the performance of schools. All of our consultants have worked recently in challenged schools and have a successful record of accomplishment improving student performance. TS specializes in assisting schools to increase academic performance in less than a year and sustain increases in three years.

ASSISTANCE PROVIDED BY TURNAROUND SOLUTIONS

- Certified and experienced team members who have recently done the work
- Personalized attention using each school's unique characteristics
- Innovative strategies to increase performance
- Tailored professional development

- Assistance to high schools with developing plans to increase graduation rates, acceleration, and college readiness
- Professional development in the areas of school and district leadership development, Common Core State Standards, family engagement, and school climate
- A variety of specialized services to charter and private schools
- Several auxiliary educational services such as college tours, lectures, labor and staffing support

SYSTEM REVIEW PROCESS

- Data management
- Assessments
- Professional development
- Family involvement
- Instructional delivery
- Lesson planning
- Master schedule
- Curriculum
- Classroom management
- Extended learning opportunities
- Attendance (student and teacher)
- Student and teacher motivational strategies
- School culture and climate
- Community outreach
- Lunchroom schedule/procedures
- Student arrival and dismissal
- Student activities
- Facility usage
- Technology

PROFESSIONAL DEVELOPMENT TOPICS

Evaluation and Alignment of Current Curriculum with State Assessment-Tested Standards

- Analysis of district curriculum to ensure appropriate coverage of standards
- Alignment of currently-used textbooks and other resources with standards
- Guidance in the implementation of Common Core State Standards
- Training on complexity and depth of knowledge as required by item specifications

In-Depth Study and Revision of Data Analysis Protocols

- Analysis of district-made and teacher-made assessments for alignment to state assessment item specifications
- Development of formative and summative assessments, as well as alternative performance tasks
- Training on implementation and use of efficient data-tracking systems, including student-driven data tracking
- Guidance in creation of focus calendars and focus lessons to address deficiencies identified through data analysis

Common Planning and Professional Learning Communities

- Collaboration with teachers to create vertical articulation of grade-level expectations
- Establishment of professional learning communities and protocols for common planning
- Guidance in the development of long-term curriculum calendars and the process of backwards planning
- Evaluation and revision (if necessary) of lesson structure/planning model

Department and Individual Professional Development Opportunities

Partial list of TS professional development topic:

- Individual coaching cycles (preconference, observation, feedback, modeling, co-teaching, debriefing)
- Collaboration with school-based instructional coach(es) to build capacity within the school
- Professional development sessions on various aspects of instruction
- Incorporating reading and writing in the content area
- Building conceptual understanding
- Implementing discovery-based learning
- Utilization of textbook resources
- Incorporating manipulatives
- Implementing a center/rotation model of instruction
- Analyzing student work to identify misconceptions
- Research-based instructional strategies
- Classroom management techniques
- Student engagement/motivational strategies
- Preparing to transition to Common Core State Standards
- Shared Inquiry
- Common Core Reading and Mathematics
- Classroom management
- Cooperative groups
- Data management
- Assessment development
- Differentiated instruction
- Hands-on investigation
- Modeling

- Preview/review
- Scaffolding differentiated instruction
- Instructional focus calendars and pacing guides
- Enrichment
- Early warning systems
- Lesson planning
- Aligning curriculum and instruction
- Curriculum mapping and pacing
- Professional development calendars
- Response to intervention (RTI)
- Teacher-student relationships

How TS Supports School Leaders

- Working with administrators to achieve annual learning gains, school improvement goals, and other targets
- Using multiple sources of data to plan and assess instructional improvement
- Improving school culture and climate
- Increasing family involvement
- Engaging staff in ongoing study of current best practices
- Accountability management
- Resource, data, and budget management
- Capacity building
- School improvement plan development
- Demanding content and instruction that ensures student achievement of established standards
- Developing skills necessary for the planning and implementation of change for effective student learning
- Hiring quality instructors

- Scheduling
- Decision making
- Assessing the curriculum needs in a particular setting
- Developing curriculum aligned to state standards based upon the needs of the students
- Creating conditions that enhance the staff's desire and willingness to focus energy on achieving educational excellence
- Developing professional learning communities

Language Arts Professional Development

- Gradual Release of Responsibility Model
- Explicit instruction
- Differentiated instruction
- Use data to guide and differentiate instruction
- Marzano's High-Yield Instructional Strategies
- Accountable talk and collaborative literature circles
- Higher-order thinking questions (Webb's Depth of Knowledge)
- State assessment writing training in scoring calibration
- Professional development in differentiated instructional lesson planning
- Assessment development and administration of quarterly timed writing assessments
- Development of progress monitoring assessments in writing, (i.e., writing portfolio and rubric creation)
- Creation of language arts curriculum guide and lesson creation resources
- Small group, teacher-led differentiated instruction lesson creation
- Facilitate intensive lesson studies to practice, reflect, and restructure
- Training in incorporating graphic organizers, thinking maps, visual aids, foldables, etc.

- Job-embedded coach modeling of best practices (coaching cycle, if applicable)
- Training in identifying target groups and instructional strategy implementation
- Development of literature circle ritual, routines, expectations, outcomes, and roles.

Science Professional Development

- Observe science teachers and provide specific strategies for improved instructional delivery
- Work with science teachers, school leaders, and regional leaders to create and improve aligned science curriculum resources
- Support science teachers by providing feedback on lessons and assessments that align with NGSSS & Common Core State Standards
- Provide national trends and best practices in science curriculum development and instructional strategy for historically underachieving students
- Secure external resources, professional development, and materials to support individual science teachers and science teams
- Serve as a coach to science teachers by providing expert advice on improving and enhancing individual lessons and units based on ongoing analysis. This will include, but is not limited to the following strategies and services:
  - Reviewing lesson plans, unit plans, and assessments
  - Understanding scope and sequence models
  - Observing classroom instruction and offering comprehensive analysis and feedback
  - Providing instructional strategy best practice training, as needed

- Supporting the development of curriculum, using the backward design model and advising scope and sequence based on essential content knowledge that addresses state and national standards
- Cultivating a standards-based, data and results-oriented culture

- Work with the academic team on design and implementation of common assessments; work collaboratively with campus-based leaders to make instructional decisions based on student performance

- Collaborate with principals in determining appropriate resources and support for teachers

- As a leader on the academic team, make recommendations on best practices for supporting curriculum alignment across all grade levels

Math Professional Development

- Professional development for the math departments can include the following topics:

- Understanding the structure of the Common Core State Standards for Mathematics

- Understanding the instructional shifts required by the Common Core State Standards for Mathematics

- Unpacking math benchmarks to identify concepts, skills, possible misconceptions, and prior and future knowledge required for student mastery

- Aligning classroom activities and assessments with test item specifications

- Analyzing the complexity and depth of knowledge of various tasks to ensure rigor

- Developing formative and summative assessments, as well as alternative performance tasks

- Implementing and using efficient data-tracking systems, including student-driven data-tracking
- Creating focus calendars and focus lessons to address deficiencies identified through data analysis, including deficiencies in prerequisite skills
- Collaborating across the math team to create vertical articulation of grade-level expectations
- Establishing professional learning communities and protocols for common planning
- Developing long-term curriculum calendars and the process of backwards planning
- Incorporating reading and writing in the mathematics classroom
- Building conceptual understanding through discovery-based learning and the incorporation of manipulatives
- Implementing a center/rotation model of instruction as a means of differentiation in the mathematics classroom
- Analyzing student work to identify misconceptions and differentiate between conceptual and procedural errors
- Utilizing research-based instructional strategies, particularly high-yield problem-solving frameworks

All TS consultants can facilitate the following training sessions:

- Stress Management for Youth
- Self-Esteem Skills for Children and Teenagers
- Dealing with School Violence: A Look at Causes and Solutions
- Developing a Positive Attitude in Children and Youth
- Teaching Youth How to Handle Differences with Other's Race, Culture and Gender
- Effective Parenting: Parent Responsibility Check-List
- Dealing with Youth's Anger and Frustration

- Interviewing Skills for Youth: Getting the Job and Keeping It
- Social Etiquette: Behavior for Specific Situations
- Developing a Healthy Home Life for Children
- Setting Boundaries for Youth
- How to Handle Situations When the Prejudice is Directed at YOU
- What NOT to say to a Child: How Words Can Damage a Child's Self-Esteem
- Developing Family Meetings: Communicating Feelings and Thoughts
- 5 Ways to Diffuse Tension: A Teenager's Guide for Cooling Off
- Dining and Social Etiquette
- Self-Confidence Building for Teens

TS will help establish a school environment that improves school safety, discipline, and family involvement.

- Attendance
- Classroom management
- Schoolwide rituals and routines
- Student Advisory Council
- Student recognition
- Student clubs
- Principal's Power Hour
- Family Coaching Night
- Student Progress Night

JAMES YOUNG, EdD

4600 Touchton Rd. E. Bldg. 100, Ste. 150 • Jacksonville, FL 32266
904-504-7299 • jyoung@turnaroundsolutionsinc.com

ACADEMIC DEGREES

University of North Florida EdD   Educational Leadership, 2007
                                        Jacksonville, Florida

Jacksonville University   MAT Educational Leadership, 1997
                                        Jacksonville, Florida

Savannah State College   BS Biology, 1991
                                        Savannah, Georgia

LEADERSHIP EXPERIENCE

President/CEO   2012 – Present
Turnaround Solutions, Inc.
- Partnership with 25 schools in 5 states to:
- Provide school turnaround services
- Increase state assessment performance in reading, math, and writing
- Increase high school performance (graduation rates, acceleration rates, and postsecondary readiness rates)
- Provide strategic professional develop, data management, and curriculum development services
- Conduct program evaluations, needs assessments, and curriculum audits

President, Turnaround Solutions Publishing   2014 – Present
Jacksonville, Florida
- Meets with key authors, content developers, and agents to assist editors in signing contracts and maintaining relationships.
- Approves contracts between the publishing house and authors, content developers, agents, and other publishers.

Principal, Ribault Senior High   2009 – 2012
Duval County Public Schools
- Increased School Performance Grade from an Intervene F to an A
- Only school in Duval County Public Schools to increase a letter grade each year

- Only nonmagnet high school in Duval to achieve an A grade
- Reading: Increased reading proficiency by 13 percentage points, overall reading gains by 21 percentage points, and lower quartile reading gains by 27 points
- Math: Increased math proficiency by 7 percentage points, increased overall math gains by 5 percentage points, and lower quartile math gains by 13 percentage points
- Writing: Increased writing level 4 or above by 34 percentage points
- Graduation Rate: Increased overall graduation rate by 17 percentage points and at-risk graduation rate by 21 percentage points
- Acceleration: Increased acceleration participation by 34 percentage points and accelerated performance by 31 percentage points
- Postsecondary Readiness (ACT and SAT): Increase PSR reading by 27 percentage points and increased PSR math by 21 percentage points
- Increased early college enrollment by 50 percent
- Student Enrollment: Increased enrollment by 250 students
- Suspension Rate: Decreased by 40 percentage points

Jacksonville University   2011 – Present
Adjunct Graduate Program Educational Leadership

Orange Park Junior High   2005 – 2009
Clay County Public Schools
- Maintained A-grade school performance for 4 consecutive years
- Reading: Increased reading proficiency by 8 percentage points, overall reading gains by 5 percentage points, and lower quartile reading gains by 4 points
- Math: Increased reading proficiency by 6 percentage points, increased overall math gains by 4 percentage points, and lower quartile math gains by 8 percentage points
- Writing: Increased writing proficiency by 8 percentage points

University of North Florida   2005 – 2009
Adjunct Graduate Program Educational Leadership

Rufus Payne Elementary   2001 – 2005
- Duval County Public Schools
- Increased school performance grade from an intervene F to an B

- Reading: Increased reading proficiency by 14 percentage points, overall reading gains by 11 percentage points, and lower quartile reading gains by 13 points
- Math: Increased math proficiency by 23 percentage points and increased overall math gains by 16 percentage points
- Writing: Increased writing proficiency by 43 percentage points

Pine Estates Elementary   1999 – 2001
Duval County Public Schools
- Increased school performance grade from an intervene F to an C
- Reading: Increased reading proficiency by 23 percentage points
- Math: Increased math proficiency by 19 percentage points
- Writing: Increased writing proficiency by 44 percentage points

PROFESSIONAL EXPERIENCE

Andrew Robinson Elementary   Vice Principal, 1997 – 1999
                                                    Jacksonville, Florida

Wolfson High School   Assistant Principal, 1996 – 1997
                                                    Jacksonville, Florida

Fletcher High School   Science Teacher, 1993 – 1996
                                                Jacksonville Beach, Florida

Winder Barrow Middle School   Science and Reading Teacher
                                                            1992 – 1993
                                                          Winder, Georgia

United States Marine Corps   1986 – 1992

PUBLICATIONS

Contributing Author. 2014. *Teenage Girls: The Guide for Health, Wellness & Self-Esteem.* Eastman, Linda Ellis, ed. Prospect, KY: Professional Woman Publishing.

Young, James. 2014. *The One-Year School Turnaround: Overcoming School Improvement Barriers Using Common Sense Solutions.* Jacksonville, FL: Turnaround Solutions Publishing.

Connect
with Dr. Young

www.TurnAroundSolutionsInc.com

info@TurnAroundSolutionsInc.com

 James Young

 @TurnaroundSI

 facebook.com/turnaroundsolutions

 jamesyoungturnaroundsolutions

social

4600 Touchton Rd. E., Bldg. 100, Ste. 150 • Jacksonville, FL 32246
f: 904-647-5092 • p: 904-504-7299

Made in the USA
Charleston, SC
22 August 2014